I0147710

# ARTIST IN A PIXILATED WORLD

## JEAN-YVES SOLINGA

## FIRST EDITION

Little Red Tree Publishing, LLC,
635 Ocean Avenue, New London, CT 06320

Previous works:

*Clair-Obscur of the Soul (2008)*
*Clair-obscur de l'âme [in French] (2008)*
*In the Shade of a Flower (2009)*
*Landscape of Envies (2010)*
*Words Made of Silk (2011)*
*Impressions of Reality (2013)*

Copyright © 2014 Jean-Yves Solinga

All rights are reserved under International and Pan-American Copyright Conventions. Except for brief passages quoted in a newspaper, magazine, radio or television review, no part of this book may be reproduced in any form or by any means, electronic or mechanical, including photocopying and recording, or by any information storage and retrieval system, without permission in writing from the publisher.

Layout and Cover Design: Michael Linnard, MCSD
Text in Forum, Times New Roman, Trajan Pro and Ariel.

First Edition, 2014, manufactured in USA
1 2 3 4 5 6 7 8 9 10 LSI 20 19 18 17 16 15 14


Front cover painting, "The Death of Sardanapalus" by Eugene Delacroix (1827).


"Transatlantic Landscapes" was first published in *Lay Bare the Canvas: New England Poets on Art* (2014) edited by Beatrice Lazarus. The Poetry Loft, Rhode Island.




Library of Congress Cataloging-in-Publication Data

Solinga, Jean-Yves
 Artist in a Pixilated World / Jean-Yves Solinga. -- 1st ed.
  p. cm.
 Includes glossary and index.
 ISBN 978-1-935656-31-9 (pbk. : alk. paper)
 I. Title.
 PS3612.A58565S77 2014
 811'.6--dc23




Little Red Tree Publishing LLC
635 Ocean Avenue,
New London Connecticut 06320
www.littleredtree.com

# Contents

## II — Flecks from Good and Evil

## III — Between Venus and Mars

## IV — In the True Garden of Eden

Epilogue:

# FOREWORD

At the risk of sounding repetitive, I say again, it is a rare occurrence indeed when a publisher begins to write a foreword to the seventh book, not least full-length book of poetry, from the same author. Such is the case with Jean-Yves Solinga's book, *Artist in a Pixelated World.* There can be few poets working today that can match Jean-Yves prolific output and at such a high quality.

The cover and title of any book, more so with a book of poetry, brings together many aspects of an author's collective thought processes, concepts and perceptions into close proximity and focus, in a visual form. What might seem to be disparate, mutually exclusive entities and concepts to the casual observer are in the mind of Jean-Yves brought together to stand logically together and in harmony.

In this case Jean-Yves has chosen Delacroix's magnificent painting, "The Death of Sardanapalus," which is a reconstructed moment in antiquity of a besieged ruler's narcissistic madness of self-destruction, together with everything around him. At first glance it might appear to be descriptive but it was perceived as highly symbolic of the French Crown, at the time, and an alarmingly dramatic depiction of the "other," the "orient," with its abandonment and erotic forms, so at odds with the ordered norms of academic approved standards of representation, and so blatantly offensive to the artificial mores of civilized French society of the early 1800s.

Note that the painting, while appearing to depict carnage of the innocents and guiltless, is disturbingly devoid of blood. Delacroix depicts a scene of bloodless terror and violence, substituting real blood with vibrant red colored elements. The painting itself and the exaggerated pixelated effect applied—highlighting of selected negative areas—is by its very nature an artistically driven decision process. The effect, in many ways, suggests modernity, in our digitized visual world, but also the conscious decision of selection by Jean-Yves in certain specific aspects. In other words the original painting, by Delacroix, is a selective interpretation of an event, symbolic and fraught with meaning—although the passing of time has robbed it of its full impact on modern eyes—and is itself selectively deconstructed and reassembled into a new visual with an additional set of meanings superimposed upon it. And as you read this book of poems, separated into loose sections for convenience, you will see the pixelated effect and selection process applied to each and every poem.

In Jean-Yves' first book *Clair-Obscur of the Soul* (2008) I wrote in the foreword that I had enthusiastically accepted his first manuscript for publication, "...because of its intensity, lyricism and insight into the essence of what it is to be human, in fact beyond and through to the heart and soul." The writing and publishing of five books, to arrive at this point, has not diminished my thought about Jean-Yves. One, at times, wonders why he has not been more widely recognized as the poet of high quality, working assiduously at his art to reach even further into the soul of what it is to live in this world.

I described Jean-Yves, in another foreword, as a "fearless," and I can think of no other fitting epithet more becoming a poet who is constantly reaching and searching for new ways to express his thoughts. Thankfully in that regard we are all the wiser, and knowledgeable, while being sublimely entertained.


Michael Linnard
New London, CT. 2014

# ACKNOWLEDGEMENT

On balance, I have been the recipient of my fair share of the riches of life; which in turn have given me the passion and need to artistically capture them. Some of these, persons and places, have thus been welcomed into my soul, never to leave. I would like to especially acknowledge my wife Elaine, my son Robert and wife Elizabeth, their son Luc as well as my daughter Nicole, her husband Marc and their daughters Noëlle and Luciana.

I would like to again extend my warmest appreciation to Michael Linnard for his gracious support throughout the years.

Jean-Yves Vincent Solinga

# INTRODUCTION

Three poems represent the verbal architecture of much of the tone of this collection: "Refusal," "The Slave that Never Was 1 & 2," and "Phantasm." My poetry allows me to take the material of reality and reconstruct it with bricks of lyricism. This process makes it possible to examine, in the density of the genre, multiple realities that are aesthetically interesting, illustrative, and may be, instructive.

Having watched my share of various reincarnations of religiously based massacres on this earth, "Refusal" gave me the opportunity to insert the reader into a seminal moment of the formation of what would become the basis for three of the major religions, Judaism, Christianity, and Islam, in the iconic person of Abraham. I, therefore, envision this prophet refusing the immediacy of killing in the same manner as that of Albert Camus who had attacked capital punishment in his writings. I see this act as a symbol of societies having alternately evolved with one less reason to kill their neighbors.

With "The Slave that Never Was I & II," I could not reconcile (even with the luxury of poetic license) which fate of the protagonist would have had the most effect and impact. Accordingly, I kept both endings. The issue is one of my major topics: Africa. The chilling success of the slave trade has changed all the facets of civilization: Cultural, Political, Legal, etc.... I therefore wanted to follow this black man from a quiet village making existentialist decisions in the early morning hours as his family disappears in the bowls of the slave trading ship. In one version he is eventually captured and will become the next body of the New World's workforce, while in the other, he will escape in the jungle and his descendants would prosper as free human beings. This second ending makes it possible to have the surrealist utopian dream of *no possible slave trade* having existed or been successful.

"Phantasm" allowed me to enter once more several worlds that make life livable: Love, art and Paris. It is not always a happy ending but the pursuit, the reconstruction; the Proustian moments make the efforts of stopping time in time with lyricism one of the joys of the genre.

The balance of the poems fall along the spectrum of envies, fears, hopes, submissive fatalism, or philosophical rebellion.

Poetry is an efficient tool to imagine a more equitable world and society "A political fable," "Five Mile an Hour Rule" or on a historical scale "The Slave that Never Was," "1492: Mea Culpa," "Constitutional Elasticity."

The icon of anti-humanism [i.e. taking man out of the equation] the digitized, interconnected, "the internet-of-everything" world, is already with us "Kafka's World," "Ad-Man goes to war," "My Refrigerator and Me." And if we cannot destroy ourselves fast enough, "No Tombstone," we will destroy things and people "Gentle Soul in the Wild," "Hotel Rwanda," "Detention Camps and Chocolate." And unfortunately, I offer very little insight as to outside help "Believers," "Atheists and Moralists," "Orphans."

With the above representative samples of a grayish-absurdist universe, I anchor my hopes on the somewhat pyrrhic victories of the routine of living with the conscience of Docteur Drieux of "The Plague," "Fragile Letters [Lettres Fragiles]," "No Need for Heroes," "The Deer Hunter," "Morality of Shades of Gray."

Ultimately, the last vestiges of any hope and fleeting happiness are where they had always been "Same Time Next Year," "Channeling Charles Aznavour," "In the Garden of Eden," "Semi-Virginal"... Moments of human joy.

The epilogue is in the form of my adaptation of Alfted de Musset's dialogue with a muse, where I reexamine the relationship between the subject of inspiration and its resulting artistic form.

Jean-Yves Vincent Solinga
Gales Ferry, CT. 2014

*« La poésie, la vraie, est dans l'harmonie des contraires. »*

Victor Hugo dans La préface de *Cromwell*


*"Poetry, true poetry, is found in the harmony of opposites"*

Victor Hugo in the Preface of *Cromwell*

# I

# PLACE CLICHY

## Place Clichy
### *A Movable Feast*

*Homage to Hemingway*

Te souviens-tu… à Clichy?
Seven meter beat keeps bouncing on the cavernous walls of his memory

Settings of quasi-Siberian cold
Early winter darkness of New England
Invaded by the gentle roundness of cobblestones from the parvis of
Notre Dame

Crescent grayish landscapes echoing under bluish crescent moons
All awash with the crimson of Parisian hedonism

Te souviens-tu… à Clichy?

Memories apparently locked in their universe
Suddenly unlocked by this seven meter beat

During his late night alchemic wizardry
Hemingway played with magic potions of eternal souvenirs
Which upon their arrival new lovers in turn rediscovered
For their intimate codified use

From the arabesque profiles of Parisian bridges against the Seine
Evaporate sweet-sour precious hours of embraces and adieu
Condensing into sugary essences in their souls

Eternal lovers' heartbeats still beating to the seven-beat cadence
Te souviens-tu... à Clichy?

*"If you are lucky enough to have lived in Paris as a young man, then wherever you go for the rest of your life, it stays with you, for Paris is a moveable feast."*

## Believers, Atheists and Moralists

The incongruity,
The instinctive and immediate confusion:

A paragraph length of dense course outline,
Offering an appetizingly tempting mixture
Of strange bedfellows and rich intermingled views,
Philosophies and personal lives.

Lives lived according to brittle nomadic tablets.
Strict strictures for daily guidance.

As well as gloriously wide expanses of autonomous possibilities.
Self-guided actions or inactions,
With only vast voids on each side as sign posts.

And yet to find out,
In the personal reflective space of a student room,
And cloyingly on the margins of the syllabus,

That, indeed, if a god there had been,

He
Would have kindly and equally
Looked down on all four of them,

For their having tried
To give a very human voice of advice... to an otherwise silent divinity.


*Remembrance of lectures on Racine, Pascal, Sartre and Camus as Moralists.*

# Waiting Room

*Discreetly looking around the room*

The sampling of old magazines was boringly predictable.
The setting a proper color of dullness.

No music playing...
Seemingly out of abundance of respect for the self-esteem of the patients.

Thoughts start to fly out of your head
And seem to crash crazily on the nondescript wallpaper.

And an overwhelming sentiment
Of absolute equality among the assembled clientele
Acted as an unsparing acidic cleansing.

This... indeed, must be the place
That best levels any pretensions
To their most elementary:
Despite our claims to cherished ideals of individuality...

... In this... a microcosm of humanity,
Between stages right and left.

Waiting a turn in our role as a colonoscopy patient.


*Seen as a staging similar to "No exit" ["Huis clos"] by Jean-Paul Sartre.*

# Sign of Life

Only one passion... Only one grandiose goal
Since his earliest training...

Confirmation...
Unquestioned, precious confirmation
The mind-expanding confirmation
Of the expected other life forms in the cosmos.

He had long ago firmly left behind
The explosive appeal of the glossy pages of science fiction of his youth.

As well as the poetic beauty of long exposure plates
Worthy of the best museum abstract paintings
Found in the digitized spins of galaxies.

Or the extravagance of movie scenarios
About the imagined surrealists societies
And the ethical hand wringing implications of extraterrestrials.

For him, those chapters had been closed
And left on the romanticized shelves
Of mankind's narcissistic gaze

Dreams such as those of the early shepherds
Inquisitively looking up as summers skies
While their herds quietly slept...
Imposing very human aspirations on stellar dust.

While now... At his feet,
Was all the living, splendidly humble confirmation he needed
In the contingency of evolutionary wizardry

... Of some sort of ant doing what ants do...

*A cosmonaut, in some distant future, taking his first look upon his first steps on the ground of a new world: He emotionally sees some sort of ant walking about and knows all he needs to know about the inherent precious significance of other lives in the universe.*

## Morality in Shades of Gray

She had been raised in a world of bright lines.
The unbroken self-assured continuity
Of abstract ethical borders.

Eternally separating the eternal good
From Omni-persistent bad choices.

From the heights of the Romanesque altar of the local church
Flowed daily rituals and yearly calendars pointing to ever mortal infractions.

Onion-skinned prayer books sat in watchful patience,
Ready to impose long judgmental protocols.

Sentences... She had always deemed appropriate
And dutifully accepted.

But for the surrealism
Of the physical and moral destruction...

The obliteration...
Of the dignity of things and people

The abject denial...
Of well-meant lessons found in the softness of nursery tales

The mental violation...
Of parental wisdom bred in the manure of men killing men.

Giving relative human splendor and majesty
To the pleasures of the flesh among the echoes of death in the streets.

*"She always remained a good mother to all her children."*
*Comment by a person who had been raised in a religious world of delineated lines*
*between right and wrong and then having gone through the daily existence of war;*
*now seeing morality in shades of gray: Such as this comment about a war bride, [her*
*upstairs co-tenant] whose husband had been sent to forced labor camp and unknown*
*fate, having a child from neighbor who had helped with her previous children.*

## Ad-Man Goes to War

Emasculated world made of bright minds,
Working in the bureau of the malleable.

Fashion industry of narcissism:
Tailoring positive images for every whim,

In this, the dangerous amoral world of success:
Based on limitless success.

Obedient service,
Offered now, by these mobilized pin-striped soldiers,

Who had previously, soullessly promoted
Empty caloric intake, self-prescription, toxic fumes and robust soap bubbles.

And now, the firm and patriotic shredding of lives.

La pub est déclarée ! 1914-1818 [The ads have been declared! 1914-1918] *A book about the very early use of media campaigns to promote public support for World War I. Book by Dider Daeninckx and shades of other promoted apologies of wars.*

# A Pixelated World: Living in a pixel

*Homage to Blaise Pascal: "The Two Infinities"*

Bluish sphere ringed by ominous darkness.
Vulnerability of apparently floating marble,
In an ocean of indifference.

The stuff of game-ball for the gods:
Furthering the diminutive inconsequential presence
Of all this humanity
Riding in seconds past the spaceship window.

And yet...
It occurred to him,
Along with a side glance... as to his place and mortality...
It occurred to him,
That billions upon billions of pixelated lives
Made up this colored entity.

And, in this canvas, within innumerable canvases,
A precious pixel existed...

That defined
Everything that would ever exist for him.

Leaving a sweet and sour taste of humbling appreciation,
Mixed with an enigmatic complexity...

In the awareness of his own infinite grandeur
And heartbreaking insignificance.

*A reflection on the iconic picture of the Earth from space in which one particular pixel would represent a singularly important being.*

# Feminine *Résistance*

Bodies and minds in foreign time warp.
Sensuality and needs
Arbitrarily suppressed by arbitrary edicts on calendar.

Bodies and minds
Reminded daily of realities:

Coffee from chestnut shells; pasta with mice feces;
Chemicals substitutes as sugar and butter.

Fresh food and milk all distant luxuries.
Gone with memories of leather soles.

Ever-present collaborationist dangers.
 Black market, jealousies and spying envies
From everyone on everyone else.

All the while the bodies and the minds
Selfishly craving for human nourishment.

Femininity...
Apparently had been put away in the closet of necessities:

Its smart cuts of coats,
                    Curvatures,
                     Rounded breasts,
                      Elegant muscular tilt of calf muscles,
                       Blushing cheeks,
                      Provocative lips,
                      And smooth legs,

All mobilized for the general good.

Leading to the astonished look,
By occupying troops in street car,

Upon the entrance of two smartly dressed women
Flaunting the passive aggressive pride and stylish appearance
Of a beaten nation.

*Inspired by an exhibit at the Musée de la résistance in Lyon, France, dedicated to the unflinching and innovative ways French women during World War II managed to use any and all material gathered by any means to fashion lines of clothing and accessories as a symbolic resistance to the "grisaille" [gloominess] under the occupation.*

## Children Appeared in the Yard

Heart breaking destruction.
Grandma's favorite chair, water logged.

Intimate violation of hurricane rain
In upper bedrooms sanctuary.

School projects and crayons...
                              And seemingly... Tomorrows...
Covered with mold.

Things and places...
              And memories...
Haunted by the nightmarish remains of sleepless nights.

Yet the universe met its match,

On that sunny afternoon filled with the joyous chirping
                              From the neighborhood children,

Playing with the spinning colored slices
Of a giant colored ball.


*Active seaside neighborhood destroyed by water and wind of a hurricane with signs of life—and especially hope—coming back under the symbol of children at play.*

## Of Royal Residues [a fable]


On a splendid day in the European dark ages,
A baby was born of a fearless leader.

Good judgment and fairness attributed to his deeds.
Strength and wisdom a combination not always coexistent:
Nothing more natural than to expect a repeat in his genes.

Wars of succession not having been very constructive:
Thus this proper, if primitive, tool for some societal decorum.

Strange, that the scientific advances of bio-discoveries
Have not led to the lie being put to this archaic belief.

That of the intrinsic, automatic and unquestioned value,
Attached by contemporary followers,
Of the modern versions of these post-birthing results.


*True believers in a republican [i.e. anti-royalist] way of governing and government,
forced to watch the uncritical sycophancy of shows based or inspired by the historical
or contemporary worlds of aristocracies or monarchies.*

# Like Greek Gods

*Air Force I.C.B.M. radar technician: "I knew that it could be my last day with my family." [Paraphrase]*

True gods... these gods of Hellenistic pretention
Living among Mediterranean marbly hills
Brighter than the static of potential nuclear clouds at their fingertips.

True god... yet with unreliable hearts of clay:
Easily invaded by susceptibilities, jealousies...
Worthy of little children...
Muddied reputations and spousal escapades of all sorts.

True gods... indeed these men-gods
Of the make-believe pages of classical academic curriculums.

These same demi-gods... with their inevitable fatal human traits
Have lived in our very earthly reality...

... In hours of long purgatories,
Surrounded by hellish dials, made of radar boredom,

With end of play scenarios,
Full of apocalyptic split-second futures.

All the while pushing their end of the scale
On which resided a wallet-picture of a family

And peripheral thoughts
Concerning infidelity and bills to pay.

*Reflections on various books about the men of the cold war era that had godlike responsibilities: these mostly anonymous men on radar screens and fingers on toggle switches, in control rooms and underground bunkers. They went to their shift with the fate of mankind at their fingertips. No need for the flowing cotton robes of Greek gods: these ordinary men had a routine breakfast with their loved ones before their shift.*

# Hotel Rwanda [redux]

*In homage to the Hotel Rwanda Rusesabagina Foundation*

The mother
Held her baby closer to her hairy chest.

The screams
From the high grass had startled her suckling toddler

The giraffe,
From up high could not ignore the blood at her padded feet,
And stopped nibbling on the tender shoots.

The elephant family
Left the convenience of the dust patch,
Stopped protecting their skins from insects bites,
And waddled majestically
past the acrid smells of burning flesh.

And thus at the asymptotes
Of animal kingdom instincts... and those of mankind...

Our kind was found to be lacking
In our precious part of precious humanity.

*The majesty of African animal wildlife in the midst of genocidal killings*

# Oil of Essence

*On the beach, Baie des anges, Nice, France.*

Floral extraction of the sensual.
Pure essence disappearing in the evening breeze.

Her body... Her soul:
The very earthly elements of sustained emotional life.

Contours of perfumed waves,
Vaporizing in the flat topography of uncaring winds,

Swirling through the unspectacular and mundane:
Through the apparent solidity of the details of existence

Sacrilegious presences... Those smells of obligations
And uncontrolled sweeps of the clock.

Overwhelming invasions from adulterated,
Unpurified Things and People.

Pellets from a dying universe,
Not worthy of this oil of distilled happiness.

Droplets of the elemental ingredients,
Made of the best memories from a revered flesh.

Now dissipated in the common air of common life:
But for these rebellious Proustian molecules.

*A whiff of "her perfume" comes across on the beach.*

## For Whom the Bell...


The walls of the room
Seemed to be respectfully quieting the world outside.

The tangle of tubing and machines
Had neatly wrapped and parked themselves.

The various harsh lights
Had now decided to spread, instead, intimate shadows.

Chairs had formed themselves in a stage-like circle:
Things and persons had taken their places for a life's last scene.

An incongruous gentle harmony flowed.

The controlled sequence of time and breathing,
Slowing at the pace of a late autumn leaf
Readying itself for its last attached-quivering.

And then... silently... so silently flow to the hardness of the floor.


*Reflections of witnessing palliative care.*

# The Microbes of the Côte-d'Ivoire

Relegated to the nomenclature of the harmful
That of organisms that subsist on scraps.

Miniscule life that exists without a presence.
Tolerated through habit.

Harmful life
Handled with the sterilized prongs of science.

Perverted metaphor represented by these children
Ironic symbiosis... these street organisms...

In the golden age of pharmaceutical discoveries.


*In the age of the best of medications of the best of human medicine, exists the "infection" of these children, called "microbes." These formers, abandoned by their parents in the Côte-d'Ivoire. Doctor Pangloss himself would have nothing to add.*

## Les Microbes de la Côte-d'Ivoire

Relégués à la nomenclature nuisible
Celle des organismes qui subsistent de déchets

Vie minuscule qui existe sans présence :
Tolérée par habitude.

Existence nuisible
Contrôlée aux pincettes stérilisées de la science.

Métaphore perverse que représentent ces enfants.
Symbiose ironique… avec ces organismes des rues…

À l'âge doré des découvertes pharmaceutiques.


*A l'âge des meilleurs médicaments de la meilleure médecine humaine, existe «*
*l'infection » de ces enfants, surnommés « microbes ». Ceux-ci abandonnés en Côte-*
*d'Ivoire. Docteur Pangloss lui-même n'aurait rien à y ajouter.*

# A Political Fable

*With gratitude to Aesop and La Fontaine*

In the gentle world of make-believe.
In fabulous stories populated by surprisingly verbal animals,
Speaking surprisingly astute and plain truths.

In a pastoral and barnyard universe.
In settings replete with quaint feathered arrogance and carnivorous
injustice.
Jalousies and edicts with panoply of malicious results
Of various innate wild life activities,

The whole affair eliciting our patronizing scoffs from the safety of our
arm chairs...

...We constructed our very own judicial surrealism
That of...

The viable entity of "three quarters of a man"
And the precious humanity of "Incorporation papers."

*Voltaire and Jonathan Swift would have been proud: Inescapable irony of the once
legal definition of a living human being as having three quarters of a vote; to the paper
entity of a corporation as deserving the same free speech rights as a person.*

## A Special Place in Hell

Imagine the surprise. Imagine the horror.
Imagine the injustice...

When mother Teresa, Gandhi,
The catholic priest volunteering to replace a Polish Jew.
The Congolese woman shielding her child
The Palestinian who had dared to fall in love with a Jew
The off duty nurse who held the dying soldier's hand...

... In an afterlife worthy of an absurdist play,

Looking to their immediate right and left
And recognizing Hitler, Stalin
Famous sadists of the tabloids
Destructors of nations, cultures, infants and families,

In an eternal limbo of judicial justice,
Waiting for an absentee judge.

*Late night Cognac induced remark by an Atheist of his frustration and only regret that, in a godless universe, there cannot exist an eternal "price" paid for evil acts on this earth.*

# God is Dead. Love is blind.

An average profession with routine expectations.
Well established limits and means to get there.

Life had become a universe of recognizable features:
Moments of feigned surprise and appreciative rictus.

All would have been well:
The zigzags of the road had been suitably fenced in,
Preventing aberrations.

———————————————————————————

Until this presence in his life,
That replaced the laws of physics by collapsing the solidity of morality

Into a singularity
Of peaceful amoral certainty and a cheerful disinterest in tomorrow.

*Watching another Franco-Italian movie of a technocrat and his office affair.*

# 1492: Mea Culpa

Irrepressible human drives.
The best and worst of human actions.
The best and worst of what we have been.

The adulterated passions... The unfiltered needs to know.

The reptilian suspicions
of that Other...
Be he our neighbor or in the tropics.

Irrational courage
Of men on flimsy boats crossing uncharted waters.
And yet, irrational fear
Of unusual ritual table habits of Ghetto family up the cobbled street.

All the while, appetite for the Other's gold in idols or tableware.

Solid entrenched justification of actions, found in dusty books,
For disregarding their claim of humanity.

The tiny cargo of these tiny ships
Had already been loaded with their future of pestilence and brutality.

The heavy chest armor
Landing on the pristine New World beaches
Was but a telling metaphor of righteous dominance
Over the hedonism of sun drenched nudity.

And any conflicted moral issues well hidden
Like the sweating flesh underneath the hard material
Fashioned from hellish heat and hammers.

While under a Mediterranean sun,
Tired centuries of questions into the nature, the integrity of that
Other's soul...

That reader of only the first half of The Book:
An irremediable proof of his unwelcomed place in proper society.

Like Quasimodo... all of these poor souls...
Bearers of the ugliness of their half-formed nature.

Irrepressible human drives.
The best and worst of human actions.
The best and worst of what we have been.

*Contingency of events on that fateful year: The decision by Spain to fund Christopher Columbus: That same year, the start of the expulsion of Jews from the Spanish state.*

# A Man of Wealth and Taste

Dangerous by what *He* represents:
Insidious welcoming of elegance of sentiments,
The ones with the attraction of the intelligent plasticity of the beauty of
the marble of museums.

*He* lays at your feet understated sexuality and sensuality:
Hints of debauched tension under a virginal reserve.

All this alluring landscape,
From the *One*,
Knowing about favoritism and favorites.
Of excellence of breeding.
Of the immortality of classic taste.
Of the purity of light... from the *Bearer* himself.

Of things absolute...
From sitting at the right side at heavenly banquets.

From his knowing how to exist on the asymptotes,
Linked incestuously to the godly,
*He* became the master of the apparently good.

*He* allows one to make genuine claims to an innocent happiness,
As you stand proudly naked in front of the altar of existential choices.

*He* brings you the magic of translucence
That allows, finally, a human knowledge of direct sight beyond the
entrance of the Cave.

*He* makes himself into any glance of his choosing,
Substituting the forgiveness of unquestioned maternal love
In all matters of other loves.

By enveloping you in his silky red cape,
*He* gives you a taste of his lofty vision,
From both the Heavenly and Hellish,
Of views reserved for pretending gods.

And for once, all of this, with a guilt free,
Outer-worldly, savory menu of choices,
Now released from any existential consequences.

He easily makes himself into the incarnation of moments of desires,
By letting *Himself* be the very substance deserving of human touch.

This... with no imposed Canons of conduct,
As *He* lets you look down on his creations within your grasp.

Like a deluded Marc Anthony, oblivious of crumbling empires,
*He* dreamily leaves you with the scent of luscious fruit on your lips,
And something about the nagging price of a missing mouthful of
dripping flesh.

*Reflections based on one of the versions of Lucifer as the favorite and most beautiful*
*fallen angel. Hence this view of the attraction of some immorality. The title is taken*
*from the Rolling Stone's lyrics.*

# Protective Fiction

*Watching the series "The Wire"*

Post-apocalyptic grandeur of urban decay.
Despair outlined by Rorschach blood stain on sidewalk.

Sprinkled like a foggy summer night sky,
Dull reflections off the expanded casings...
From a thirty-eight special.

Sharp anguish defined by infected needles.
Multi-purpose bed sheets, of equal filth,
For lovemaking or dying.

Greek chorus urgency of screaming police sirens.
Gauntlet of life or death's primordial instinctive reactions,

Followed by perceived disrespectful looks,
Stray bullet stream,
All of it with existential results.

Nightmarish world... Abandoned by the Devil himself.
Cinéma vérité of the gut-wrenching
Abuse of the senses,
Abuse of the body.

Opiate-fed dreamscapes and illusions,
Temporarily embraced and discarded,
Of an Eden found in the creases and crevasses
Made of human flesh.

Meticulous Hollywood reconstruction
Of this foreign land and language,
Of a world of misery, safely distant from our backyard.
For the jaded armchair Ebenezer among us.

———————————————————————

Suddenly, a knot of guilt seizes the once jaded viewer.

And despite its veils of protective fiction
Nothing can dilute the Dickensian horror
From the acrid smells emanating from these,
The descendants of racial diaspora.

*Uncomfortable awareness of guilt, the viewer has, watching the retched and racist world of urban life in the quasi-fictional series "The Wire."*

## Genesis Man

It was the morning after:
The Rubicon had been crossed.

Things, people and the thereafter had been existentially committed..

Five star generals had done it before:
With human reluctance and appropriate trepidation.

On a rainy late spring day,
With no one to share the burden in that G.I. tent.

---

And so, on this morning of razor-edge defeat,
Of a seemingly bloodless academic affair,
Of a battle won and lost.

Ballot boxes full of metaphors for bullets and canons.

In the seemingly grandiose ambivalence of,
One man for another.
One view for the other one.
One temperament instead of that one.

Leaving you looking into the mirror,
With that symbolic razor.

*Reflections on the consequences of Ralph Nader's candidacy.*

# Unending Evolution

Alfred Nobel and his invention, stand as the song bird in the mine:
Back breaking work, with metal rods and hammers,
Sent to the museum glass cases of labor tools.

Leaving behind explosive forces,
The like of which had never been seen outside of the bad temper of nature.

Dominion of the earth had been henceforth
Passed on to mankind, as divinely prescribed.

Mountains would be traversed
Efficient commerce and social communication could not be far behind.

...Along with more effective killing in the trenches of infamy.

---

This thought comes to mind, as we smugly enter
From the convenience of our homes,
Our far-away bank account,

Presently flashing a zero balance.

And the winning foot prints, in the modern-day mud,

Of a Darwinian hacker.


*Humankind seems unfortunately condemned to bringing the worst aspects of our natural competitiveness into our distant future: Thus perverting, as soon as it is invented, every new idea, ostensibly designed for human advancement.*

# II

# FLECKS FROM
# GOOD AND EVIL

# Flecks from Good and Evil

*Gray souls in a gray universe*

Youth is one victim of time:
Illusions the other.

Icons of this earlier innocence
Become brittle and show previously unnoticed fissures.

The magical generosity of Santa Claus
Had, in fact, been paid in the precious money
Borrowed from the simplicity of childhood:

The unblemished image of a father painted by the family apologizers:
A serial abuser hidden behind an unsteady mask
In the boozy vapors of holiday gatherings.

The scandalous divorce of our sweet kindergarten teacher
Gave us hints of very human weaknesses in matters of love.

The sharply delineated extremes of ethics of bible studies
Proved themselves, in sleepless nights,
To be only well intentioned moral lessons

While... on the side of the reality of life...

... Flecks from Good and Evil had been sprinkled
Into the continuous spectrum
That are the nuances of human souls.

Nuances, often shaped by moral tremors of conscience in adults
Who continue to search the empty sands of absurdism for absolutes:

Leaving us looking for a measure of redemption, great or small,
Sometimes found in the incongruous intimacy
Of a tear-soaked acknowledgment of a death bed. *

*... of a conjugal bed. [Alternate endings]*

# Dream Sequence: Living in a Perfect World

It had finally happened.
Mankind had done it!
Technically. Scientifically. Biologically.

Humanity had become the summit of ideal relationships.

In the controlled environment of earth.
In the absolutely safe urban streets.
In the impeccable matching of mates and careers.

Anxieties and social unknowns had been eradicated.
Rape, murder, incivilities of all sorts and types,
Sent to the archives of real-politick and scandalous news.

Unlike Candide's ironic surroundings,
Of pain and mayhem,
This was indeed the "best of best worlds".

---

He woke up from this dream in a cold sweat of realization
That the appearance of paradise would be a world
Of nightmarish, crushing boredom.

For that is when he measured
The impact for this sort of absolute quietude
On the quirks of the human spirit.
Evolution was indeed still in our veins.

Darwinism with its diabolical attraction:
To chance and game.
The conquest and the chase

The tension of the sensual and sexual.
The prettiest plumage or shapelier derrière.

The blood pumping excitement of razor-edged decisions.
The gentle perversion from bending of rules

The multiplied permutations of unknown outcomes

Of living in gloriously tacky, shades of gray.

*"The Stepford Wives" gone global.*

# The Fawn, the Mother and Existentialism

*"Go, gentlemen. One second!*
*On your way out, take the passage to the left.*
*In the one on the right I've posted some guards*
*in order to assassinate you."*
*"Caligula," Act 3 scene 1*

Not often do the gods come to the commonplace that is ours.
A mere curvy back road:
Between routine work and sleep

A dull, mindless daily ride
Between boredom and something less.

And so... the divinities care to intervene.
Deign to make their powers known once again.

---

A clueless fawn is standing fearlessly frozen in the road,
Its mother, motherly watching.

With the sound of a car and the future approaching,
The microcosm of the scene becomes humanity's symbolic fate:

One in which,
A step to the left or right is unfortunately the choice to forever.

*Watching a fawn in the roadway as a car is arriving around the corner. Echoes of a scene from the play by Albert Camus,"Caligula," where the Caesar of Rome takes on the arbitrary role of a god.*

# A Clear Conscience

*Homage to Victor Hugo's Le mendicant (The Beggar)*

No immediate explanation from his heart
But it kept him glancing into the rearview mirror
With an incongruous feeling of sappy bitter tenderness.

Why would, on this day... this scene,
Bother his comfortable commute?

---

Pastoral surroundings.
Iconic little pond with prerequisite urban ducks.
High bourgeois life.
Well-toned newly minted mothers pushing high tech Swedish strollers.

A just and constructive life:
Earned going over obscure legal precedents on eve of bar exam.
And still, this irritating knot in his throat.

---

He had, once again, passed by the invisible trash collecting crew,

When,
Proudly smiling in front of the refrigerator,
With a good day's accomplishment,
And covered with lung-destroying dust,

An image of his father, coming home,
Had bled through the filter of righteousness
Into his reality.

## Of Form and Substance

It must have happened on some shaded patio,
And a cool lemonade away from the Southern heat.

Among the elongated vowels of the natives,
Still immensely proud of their native son.

It must have been then, that an inspired artist
Originally put the iconic posture of Elvis Presley on velvet.

The rest is mindless repetitive history.

Thus is the cryptological rendering of poetry,
In purposefully jumbled sentence structures,
As proof of intellectual headiness.

Not unlike a thoughtful expression and its individual words
Randomly pulled out of a paper bag.

Then proudly and sequentially presented
As some alchemic proof of inspiration.

*The shameless production and reproduction of so called "Velvet Elvis Paintings"
and the various attempts to outdo E.E. Cummings into poems of weirder and weirder
shapes.*

*With echoes of "Le bourgeois gentilhomme" of Molière where the character is amazed
with himself after realizing that he has been speaking in a form called "prose."*

# Cemented Prejudice

*The sloping arches of the Long Island parkways bridges*

Not unlike generals at their wooden tables,
With their lifeless iconic toy soldiers
As stand-ins for the realities of flesh on the eve of battle.

Arranging and re-arranging with heartless precision
The colored specks on the campaign maps.

Men of Pharaonic visions
Invading the intimate lives of future generations.

Visions of concrete and metallic spans:
Pushing and herding urban humanity,
At the point of an architect's stylus.

Invading their existence, in an existentialist way,
With shards of longer commute, circuitous distances to hospitals
And anonymously missed parent-teacher meetings.

Did the huddled masses of Ellis Island
Quitclaim their inheritance to the cooling ocean breezes
Upon renting their fifth floor tenement,
Full of the vapors of the ethnicities of cuisines?

Were these close-knit neighborhoods
-Emotional ancestors to us all-
Shelved in the dusty archives of history,

Along with the ideals
Of a land of the tired... for the tired... and the reshuffled?

*Urban builder and planner Robert Moses (often compared to Baron Haussmann
of Second Empire Paris fame) whose vision and decisions had practical and daily*

*human consequences, such as the displacement of whole ethnic neighborhoods. And then, what about the still controversial extreme sloping design of the arches over the original stretches of the Long Island parkways which, as urban folklore would have it, were so designed to make access to the beaches more difficult by buses from the urban areas. Whether this is calumnious or not, it was hinted in contemporaneous articles and is unfortunately still repeated and says something about depth of social wounds.*

## My Refrigerator and Me
The internet of everything


Lucifer was a good judge of character:
The apple at the end of the bargain had to be spectacularly juicy.

The price to be paid well worth the pound of flesh.
The inconvenience, intelligently hidden
In the flowing flowers of endless fields of happiness.

Social intercourse became miraculously instantaneous and unerring.

As so much Manna with an impeccable social approval,
The biblical temptation of the internet of everything
Came to pass by showering goodness on everything.

No one was left out: For no-where to hide
Absolute interconnectivity.

Answers given to as yet unformulated questions.

Indeed, Doctor Pangloss would have been flustered with envy,
In this, the best of the best of worlds.

_____

Which sounded hollow to this husband, as his wife's divorce lawyer
Displayed on the court's giant screen
The barcode of his mistress's prescription medicine
Recorded by the refrigerator's memory
After her week-end visit.


*Eventual consequences of house appliances linked to the internet.*

# Alternate World

On that primordial morning,
In the humid vapors of toxic volcanic fumes
And trembling vibrations of gigantic beasts,

Life of all shapes and spans
Was doing what evolution whispered in its brain.

Unending mayhem of shredded body parts and blood baths.
Disemboweled entrails and death stares.

Drowning mammals and suffocating mothers.
Dying screeches of all sorts yelling their doom to a deaf surrounding.

Arbitrary life or death results for stepping to the left.
And ensuing imposition of multiple mates.

Life, then, was dictated according
To an amoral obedience to blind survival.

In a Darwinian garden of natural laws
Sprinkled in a natural universe.

A setting outside of the borders of ethics,
Unaffected by reflections upon superior codes of good conduct.

———————————————————

Since that early morning
Bathed in its reddish-white light in the sky,

Since that moment of existence-altering dimension
From errant exploding asteroids,

Mankind was handed its second chance
In fashioning its own existentialist-driven destiny.

A path...
Arguably containing a modicum of dignity of purpose.

The latter seemingly absent
In light of the still present, blood-covered body parts
In the streets of too many cities.

*Newscasts full of unending violence leading to the philosophical speculation about a world where Homo-sapiens would not have survived the asteroid strikes and had left the earth to lower sentient animals.*

# Constitutional Elasticity

Visions of a tired humanity
Stepping from the bending planks of a minuscule boat,
Unto the virginal spaces of New England.

These families, full of corporal wariness in their limbs.
But hopeful blank-slates of potential in their minds.

Could it indeed come to be true again
That previous mistakes of the past
Would have been carried in the seeds of similarity in their pockets?

Thus re-seeding the crab-grass of the most iconic of tyrannies:
That of an imposed presence in one's heart and thoughts?

---

What a vision for an antidote to this temporary fever:
The Oh! ... So gently and doubly symbolic response...

That of a quiet reading of a splendidly wide-opened,
Noisy, pulpy, pre-tablet, New York Times Newspaper

During the 'Non-unconstitutional'
Recitation of an opening prayer!

*Written with the fervent hope that the future reader will find this topic just a quaint footnote of history: in this case, the Supreme Court's decision that a northern New York State city is within constitutional understanding of the separation of Church and State in opening its sessions with a prayer.*

## Dark Ages Revisited

Dark ages invading our conscience.
Like uncivilized mores imposed on living room luxury
By uncouth marauding attackers

Imposition on our tranquility:
This unspeakable mindless neglect of brotherly flesh.

Time-warp display
Of third-world subhuman dimensions:

This miracle of technology...
Taking the viewer effortlessly to a co-existing scene,
Comfortably hiding behind the flatness of the screen.

Faithful technological representation in living colors
Of mud incrusted eyes and emaciated children..

World of Dickensian honesty
And picture-perfect description of the dismal science.

Seemingly miraculous cinematographic reconstruction
Of centuries past: Unfiltered. Uncut. Uncensored.

The real obscenity of real life:
Children working in mercury-filled mud pits
For nuggets of gold.

Miracle of technology! This time machine.
Direct live pictures from Hell:

A step away from the television control.

*African children working with picks in open-sky digs for specks of gold: Amidst mercury fumes, the fatalistic widow mother of six children.*

# Bare Stones

Wisdom entered the soul that day...

Not with the sound of virile trumpets.
And not through the opaque syllogisms of philosophy.

No circular ethics rebounding off the doubting of morality.

And most of all... Not through the imposition
Of inquisitional regurgitation of partially digested chapters
On humanity's standing among Things

---

No... Nothing but a pastis-drenched lunch.
The Provençal heat and the ever-present echoes of cicadas.

And...
The enduring majestic nudity of the stones of the Orange Theatre,
Bringing us back to where we ultimately belong:

On the continuum of ephemeral center-stage appearances.

*Reflections on the Roman Amphitheatre in Orange, France and a Gallic nod to the omnipresent Shakespeare.*

# Orphans

Life had tried... To instinctively and ever so carefully
Attach itself.

From its inception...
Febrile fertilized cells on the walls of maternal moistness.
Followed by tenuous symbolic umbilical links:
To be symbolically cut
To establish some degree of cherished freedom.

We then endeavor to form a multitude of spiraling cocoons of relationships:
Legal and emotional ties of all sorts.
To others, to things... to arbitrary dates in calendars and sweeping clicks
on office clocks.

Iconic and symbolic alter-egos of all sorts and constructs,
Found in the glue of religions, languages and cultures:

Thus creating anchors for our images on Others:
In the moving sands of delusions.

But whether king, queen or emperor;
Prime minister or page-one idol
Leader of mankind with the megaphone of oratory
Or forgotten follower in the muddy trenches of history
Activist mayor or his disillusioned street-sweeper,

We will each finish the last breath of our last day...
Whether accompanied, admits collective tears
Or with just an inquisitive street dog sniffing at our cooling flesh,

By terminating our presence on this world
The way it had been entered

As an orphan...
Made so, by an absent universe,
Unaware of its parenthood.

*Born in a universe where all of us are born orphans.*

## Gentle Soul in the Wild

Strange whiteness…
This marbly smoothness of pelt
On this creature in their midst.

Quiet gentle presence
Witness to their secretive daily routines.

Primordial wild pounding of chest.
Unscripted reconciliations and rituals.

Sounds of verbalized satisfaction
From lyrically cinematographic mating under the spring rains;
And birthing under the shiny green privacy of leaves.

Suspicious clicking of magic black box,
Eternalizing the surprising fragility of tender moments,
Among incredibly powerful, unforgiving arms.

She had become the accepted presence
Of a family's crazed but harmless aunt.

She had entered their world with the magic key
That all good strangers use to enter the home of strangers:

The reciprocal, respectful acceptance
Of the values of the Other.

*Unabashed anthropomorphism: The murder of Dian Fossey foremost renowned primatologist in the mountains of Rwanda as if witnessed by the very gorillas she had studied and protected.*

## Possession

*Sunset on the Pont des Artistes in Paris*

He did not want to kiss her.
He did not want to hold her in his arms.
Nor did he want to read his presence as a reflection in her eyes.

He needed to be instead
    *possessed*
        by her lips,
            her arms,
                and her glance.


## Possession

*Couché de soleil sur le Pont des Artistes à Paris*

Il ne voulait pas lui donner un baiser.
Il ne voulait pas la tenir dans ses bras.
Il ne voulait non plus pas lire son propre reflet dans ses yeux.

Il avait plutôt besoin d'être
    *Possédé*
        Par ses lèvres,
            Ses bras,
                Et son regard

# A Book's Cover

Teacher... students love to hate.
Infamous name mentioned in cafeteria line:
With post- residue syndrome of angst and loathing.

Inflexibility of persona,
Putting in doubt his very humanity.

Had he ever had a nice word?
Did he sleep in a coffin?

Who would have married him anyway?
No wonder he taught math... he thought it was romantic!

---

Then a random television coverage
About random acts of kindness.

And the same astonishing figure:
That same stern stature and awkwardness of the man,
With vague aspects of retired Marine drill-sergeant.

Dressed in the incongruity of hospital whites,
Inside the surrealism of a post-natal intensive care unit.

Gently, so gently... whispering to a baby.
The stone-faced taskmaster had the appearance
Of holding a sacramental offering
In the cottony softness amidst his muscular protection.

An unshakable substitute for a mother's love:
Holding quasi-religiously, in its very fragility,
An image of human kindness.

*Inspired by a true story (with some poetic license)*
*Unlikely strict and burly math teacher caught doing pro bono visits for sick or*
*motherless babies in hospital. [February 14, 2014. CBS news*

## The Slave That Never Was I *

There had been rumors for days.
The rumors turned into black clouds of burning huts from the West.

To the crescendo of sporadic screams reflecting from the hills.
To the children huddling a little closer around the night fire.

He had heard of families disappearing.
Sometimes only crying babies, sick elders
And pathetic women in labor left behind

It seemed that these particularly smart evil spirits,
Dressed in foreign cloth and speaking in guttural barks
*Wanted only the best of the land*

———————————————————

In the fog of sleep and blood-chilling agony,
He was unable to grab any of his children.

And only basic survival instincts
Led to his running to the favorite fishing spot,
On a secluded sharp curve in the river.

There... to be witness to the parting
Of worlds and civilizations.

That day... in the early mist.
On the river that had fed his own.

To the chorus of screams from the boats,
Of a humanity decreed to help built a New World.

The infernal equation intimately balanced
By the dead sailor who had stood in his way.

*\* There are two versions to this poem because of the seminal differences in the pro-
tagonist's act.*

*Envisioning a black tribal villager running through the village to escape the slave-
traders who are rounding up their next cargo. He fights and never becomes the slave
he was intended to be.*

# The Slave That Never Was II *

There had been rumors for days.
The rumors turned into black clouds of burning huts from the West.

To the crescendo of sporadic screams reflecting from the hills.
To the children huddling a little closer around the night fire.

He had heard of families disappearing.
Sometimes only crying babies, sick elders
and pathetic women in labor left behind

It seemed that these particularly smart evil spirits,
Dressed in foreign cloth and speaking in guttural barks
Wanted only the best of the land

---

In the fog of sleep and blood-chilling agony,
He was unable to grab any of his children.

And only basic survival instincts
Led to his running to the favorite fishing spot,
On a secluded sharp curve in the river.

There... to be witness to the parting
Of worlds and civilizations.

That day... in the early mist.
On the river that had fed his own.

To the chorus of screams from the boats,
Of a humanity decreed to help built a New World.

* There are two versions to this poem because of the seminal differences in the
protagonist's act.

Envisioning a black tribal villager running through the village escaping only
momentarily the slave-traders who are rounding up their next cargo.

# Five Miles an Hour Rule

*Driving while black*

For the common man... The iconic symbol.
The feel of freedom in the steering wheel.

Just some metal and rubber tires:
And yet surprisingly democratizing.

Freedom of all sorts.
For all type of behaviors and misbehaviors.

Wide-opened spaces and four wheels to get you there.
No more walls.
And the space in which to know the joy,
The chase, the pursuit... Of quasi-constitutional happiness.

Driving implied the unbeknownst existentialist moment
Of choosing left from right:
Wondering for years over the significance.

A movable living room for the blue collar to breathe.
The college freshman to look at his past
One more time through the back window.

And his first unknowing glance
On his future spouse on the college lawn.

Unfortunately we seem to have also found space in the trunk
For the dirty linen of racial profiling.

For what should rightly have been
The innocent metaphor
Of a nation's youthful innocent exuberance and unbridled energy.


*Contrasting the liberating imagery of road travel in Jack Kérouac's work and this commentary by an African American more than a generation later: "You learn to move slower," referring to the speed limit. He called it the "5 mph rule." He had learned to go that much slower than any posted speed limit. (Comment by middle class black man and his memories of surviving in parts of the U.S.)*

# Fragile Letters *

*To Noëlle*

Curved scrapings into the bark of the biggest plane tree
Will lose the shape of precious names with every season.

The same as names written with strong reeds of Camargues
In the wet sands of the indigo Mediterranean:

Giving these fragile letters their tender arrogance.

All these attempts are no more than messages in a bottle,
Thrown into the future unknown,

Hoping that they will be read by the knowing fingertips,
Made of the flesh of our flesh…

Who will recognize in the remaining wavy folds
The remnants of our loving protective presence for you.

*Thoughts on First Grand Child*

* *First published in English in* Words Made of Silk (2011)

## Lettres Fragiles

Les grattures arrondies dans l'écorce du plus grand platane
Perdront leurs formes des noms précieux avec chaque saison.

De mêmes les noms écrits avec les durs roseaux de Camargue
Dans le sable mouillé du bleu indigo de la Méditerranée.

Donnant à ces fragiles lettres leur tendre arrogance.

Tous ces efforts ne sont que des messages dans une bouteille,
Jetée dans l'inconnu du futur.

Espérant qu'ils seront lus par des doigts savants,
Faits de la chair de notre chair…

Qui reconnaîtra dans les plis restants
Les traces de notre affectueuse présence protectrice

*Pensées pour notre première petite-enfant, Noëlle.*

**Phantasm**
Between Le Louvre and Clichy


Witnessing a virgin... where once stood a woman.

Transmutation of the pulsating carnal knowledge
Into an untouchable and untouched ideal,
Found high above and behind the altar of reclaimed self-restrain.

A wounded soul looking for the salvation of self-worth
In the post paradisiac setting of Parisian streets.

Witnessing a virgin... across the café table
of Le départ de Saint Michel,

Against her halo background effect
Created by the silhouette of Notre Dame de Paris,

Symbolized by the confusion of cross-currents
From the moist echoes of passion
In the still delectable hints of a smile on her lips.

Grandiose, noble and generous ambivalence
Of all that is splendidly divine in the flesh;
And human in our dreams.

Not unlike the experience of virtual vertigo on early morning walks
In an empty Louvre:

Looking, with gulps of sad envy, upon the beatitudes
Of the transcended flesh of biblical serenity...

That place in art, where a momentary balance is created,
At the tip of the artist's feverish touch,
Between the now and the forever.

Tearful in front of Renoir's unblinking animal desires
For an insatiable physical possession of searing photons...

For what André Gide would call the frustration of sight.

The ethereal nobility of carnal presence in paintings
Co-existing in his memory with acrid smells of faded petals of lubricity,
Left in a miniscule third floor in Clichy

Overlap of past and present,
In the nuptial hints of wrinkled sheets,
Between a nineteen sixties bed of counter-culture
And that of the shades of lithium whiteness in Manet's Olympia.

Stains of memories like so much organic remnants of living cells,
As lingering traces of humid happiness, invading his walk
On the uneven cobbles stones on the way to Le Pont des artistes.

---

She carries now the aura of an illuminated Madonna
Found in the smoky gothic side chapels of l'église Saint Germain-des-prés

She stands, immobile, made of the bluish and white colors of Italian marble,
In glorious ambivalence,
As the mother of God and goddess of us all:

Safely, emotionally and irrevocably out of reach,
With parapets of white stone marking the inviolate space
In the shadows of the déambulatoire.

This is where...
He is driven to the unthinkable... the damnable
The shameful hypocrisy and telling despair

Of noisily dropping coins, in order to light a quaint candle,
To this woman...
Fashioned in the coldness of stone, the limpidity of painterly oils
And the furnace of a knowing flesh.

While at other times hiding her contours of pink skin
Discernible under the vaporous pigments of renaissance magic

In the mannerism of Athena

She would, at times, allow hints of a mere human presence
Under folds of the translucence of cotton,

All this magic capturing in his soul
The generous complexity and unapproachability

Of desires.

*The oscillating visions between the quasi-virginal unapproachability and sulfurous*
*sensuality in the same woman.*

**Phantasme**
Entre le Louvre et Clichy

Voyant une vierge… là, où se trouvait jadis une femme.

Transmutation de la pulsation charnelle
En un idéal intouchable et hors du tactile
Se trouvant au-dessus et un peu à l'arrière d'un autel :
Avec une réserve retrouvée.

Une âme blessée, cherchant le salut de l'amour-propre
Dans le paysage post-paradisiaque des rues parisiennes.

Voyant une vierge… en face de la table d'un café
Du *Départ de Saint Michel,*

Contrastant avec l'effet auréolé
Formé par la silhouette de Notre Dame de Paris,

Symbolisée par l'alliance des contre-courants
Des échos humides de la passion
Dans les indices encore délicieux d'un sourire sur les lèvres.

Grande ambivalence, noble et généreuse,
De tout ce qui est splendidement divin dans la chair
    Et humain dans nos rêves.

Un peu comme ce sentiment de quasi-vertige durant des randonnées
matinales dans un Louvre vide :

En observant, avec un triste sentiment d'envie sur le cœur,
Les images de béatitudes de la chair transcendées en sérénité biblique.

Ce lieu artistique… où l'art,
À la pointe du touché fiévreux de l'artiste,
Crée, entre le présent et l'éternel, un moment d'équilibre.

Pleurs, aux yeux grands ouverts,
Face aux désirs primordiaux d'un Renoir
Qui cherchait tant à satisfaire son insatiable besoin

De possession  de photons cautérisant :

Pour soigner, ce qu'André Gide appelait la frustration du regard.

La noblesse éthérée de la présence charnelle des tableaux
Coexistant dans le souvenir, parmi les odeurs âcres de pétales fanés de
lubricité,
Oubliés dans un troisième étage minuscule de Clichy.

Superposition du passé et présent
Dans les indices nuptiaux des draps froissés,
Entre un lit de contre-culture des années soixante
Et ceux de nuances de blanc lithium de l'Olympia de Manet.

Taches de souvenirs, comme celles des restes de cellules vivantes,
Comme traces persistantes d'un bonheur humide, envahissant son par-
cours Sur les pavés inégaux, en allant vers le Pont des artistes

---

Elle porte maintenant l'aura d'une illumination de la Madone
Trouvée le long des chapelles gothiques enfumées de Saint Germain-des-
prés.

Debout, immobile, faite d'un marbre italien
Aux couleurs bleuâtres et blanches,
De cette glorieuse ambivalence,
De la mère de Dieu et déesse de nous tous.

À l'abri,
Émotionnellement et irrévocablement hors de notre portée,
Avec des parapets de pierre blanche démarquant  l'espace inviolable

Dans l'ombre des déambulatoires de l'abbaye

C'est là…
Qu'il est poussé à l'inconcevable... au blasphème
À la honteuse hypocrisie et l'évident désespoir,

En laissant tomber bruyamment des pièces de monnaie
Pour après allumer une mignonne bougie

Au nom de cette femme…

Construite de la froideur de la pierre,
La limpidité des huiles de tableaux
Et du feu de la chair avertie.

Alors qu'elle cache des fois ses contours d'une peau rose
 Perceptible dans les teintes de la magie de la Renaissance.

À la manière d'Athénée
Elle permettait des fois de montrer de petits soupçons de présence
humaine
Sous les plis translucides de coton,

Toute ces images incorporant dans son âme
La généreuse complexité et l'inapprochable…

Des désirs.

*Le vacillement de visions entre l'intouchable quasi virginité et la sensualité sulfu-
reuse chez la même femme.*

# III

# BETWEEN
# VENUS AND MARS

## Between Venus and Mars:

*Of Simone de Beauvoir and The Stepford Wives*

Between innocence and the void left on the heart by time...
Are the ripples of wisdom on the soul.

They are found in the late of night...
In conversations under the harsh lights and meaningless frigid cups of coffee.

This is where very specific questions are answered by crumbling sentences...

Followed by evading glances toward the blackness of the windows
That show disappearing reflections of a vaporous couple.

---

She had believed in wedding vows and white veils
That foretold of a uniformity of life toward happy endings:

While reality is more often in muddy shades of grays and runny pastels,

Until... all that is left of innocence
Will be streaks on a moist and wrinkled paper handkerchief.

Between the perfect soufflé and the melted candles
Exists a perfect meal....
Pregnant glances and anticipated moments
Measured by sensual bites of melted Brie and the flint bouquet of a Chablis.

Between a slow dance to Moon River and awakening to Coming Around Again
Lives the unraveling of the concept of perfection.

Innocence... like a valued family crystal
Shattering into pieces on the solidity of the reality of kitchen tiles.

These same tiles that knew a softer beginning in the moistness of clay
Before being kilned into and for the hardness of the world.

If only we could find the proper furnace to steel our heart and soul...
Rendered soft from their splendid years of youth and innocence...

... In order to prepare them
Against the opaque solidity we call reality.


*Reflections on the clear-eyed persona of Simone de Beauvoir versus the women of The Stepford Wives.*

*To the music of Carly Simon's "Coming Around Again."*

# Recycled

Some concepts are too broad
Some dangers are too abstract.

Probability is that
 It... Won't happen to us.

It... Happens somewhere else, to someone else.

We have had... It... Around all these years.

We will still produce more of... It.

It... Is not to be seen, nor smelled.

Asteroids are more concrete:
The stuff of thrills. Good sciences fiction. Good horror stories.

_____

But once in a while.... From the bowels of the earth,
Things have a way of talking to us,

Using the scatological vocabulary,
That had so much captured our attention in our youth:

That of...
Ca-ca... Poo-poo

*Reflection on the report of a new form of cholera that had spread after an outbreak in the Americas. It had started in Haiti as a result of substandard waste controls by United Nations "Blue Helmets" on the island. This strain of cholera spread to the continent in Mexico. Prompting this remark: "This is a concrete example of how the earth is indeed a closed system. If we don't take care of our shit, we will end up eating it."*

# New England Sun

Pellets of a watery Universe.
Bursts of brutish forces.
Spins of molecules giving form to emotions.

Palette of nuances,
From vaporous whiteness...
To transparent artic blues,

Making for introspective reflections
Of hidden multiplicity full of thriving life
Under the cloak of the pure energy of Things.

All under the diffused photons of a stormy light
With dispersed patches of browns,
Offering hints of a random organic earthiness:

Iconic symbols of the ingredients
Of mankind's genesis.

*Reflections upon photograph taken late autumn on National Seashores, Cape Cod*
*(Tumultuous wave action, shy sun and beach sand interspaced in the cold rollers).*

# Transatlantic Landscapes*

*"Late Afternoon (Sunset)," by Frederick Childe Hassam (Florence Griswold Museum, Old Lyme, Connecticut)*

Nature's quiet misty dignity
Covering the stateliness of Things,

Entered through the multiple translucent screens
Made of lacy shyness.

Silky veils made of layered feathering.

Touches...
Giving the sun the timid reserve of a sleepy celestial vestal.

Wavelets of pale blues and tea-greens,
Wistfully supporting a palette
Of marine mauves and dying embers of earth tones.

Statement in muted un-verbalized lyricism
About the universal and the human gaze:

All in the rich nuances of esthetic fraternity.

*Reflection of the influence of Claude Monet on Frederick Childe Hassam and some of their artistic convergences.*

*First published in* Lay Bare the Canvas: New England Poets on Art (2014), *edited by Beatrice Lazarus. The Poetry Loft, Rhode Island.*

## Grayish Vapors of Reality

Shards of guilt...

Purity of intense light beam searing the living flesh,
Between mounds of quivering molecular memories.

Parental childhood echoes
Of reprimands and reminders for pristine actions.

Unspoiled illusions of the Good's mission
In somehow diluting the Bad.

What now of this youth,
Nourished by the integrity of Things in the universe?

Things, in an adolescent world,
Near at hand and concrete in his soul?

Calling balls and not out?
Turning down cheat-sheets?

Intimacies not divulged?
Urges not imposed?

Destructive rumors not repeated?
Weaknesses not abused?
Introverted strengths gently applauded?

---

Indeed a true apostle of the righteous path,
Doing his part in the living world,
For a hopeful goal of a better world.

Did his conscience get the best of him,
While the Other slept deeply at night?

Not able to reconcile the personal collective guilt
Of living in a parasitically collective happiness?

*A writer's ethics at odds with his relationship to the military industrial complex*
*suspected as factor in his suicide.*

## The Symbol of Things Good

It is a moment when we profess our creed:
That the child is… indeed, the best link in the best of worlds.

He is the symbol of the strength of Good
That surprises us in the fragility of birth.

He is the light in the darkness
Contradicting some of the pages of history.

His presence, full of futures, melts the obstacles to the fullness
of human happiness…
… Man-made and otherwise.

He is the bundle of reconciliation of Things and People
Representing the emotional and lasting sheen
In the diversity of the mosaic of life.

He will remain, in the warm protective glance of those
Who have lovingly, carefully and emotionally swaddled him.


*To my grandson.*

*First published in English in* Words Made of Silk (2011)

# À Luc

C'est le moment où l'on professe notre crédo:
Que l'enfant est... vraiment la meilleure liaison dans le meilleur des
mondes.

Il est le symbole de la puissance du Bien
Qui nous étonne parmi la fragilité de la naissance.

Il est la lumière dans le noir
Contredisant certaines pages de l'histoire.

Sa présence, remplie de futurs, fait fondre les obstacles menant au
bonheur humain...
.... Que ceux-ci proviennent de l'homme ou de parts ailleurs..

Il est entouré du coton de la réconciliation entre les Choses et les Hom-
mes,
Représentant la patine émotionnelle et dure
Dans les nuances de la mosaïque de la vie.

Il continuera dans le regard doux et protecteur de ceux
Qui l'auront tendrement, soigneusement et émotionnellement protégé.

« *The Symbol of Things Good* » *en anglais*

## No Need for Heroes

Generations of still fidgety elementary classes
Faced with byzantine minutiae of byzantine ancestors.

Images and sounds amazingly digitized and reconstructed.
Sensory smells of quaint old ways and manners.

Wasteful consumption and ridiculous locomotion.
Lough out-loud clothing and circus-like hair styles.

Omnipresent diseases fearfully around us and in us
Miseries of climatic ill-temperaments imposed on us

Tells of horrors of famines and collapsing infrastructures
Colliding cars and planes
And other seemingly fatalistic and now...
Fantastic happenings

But nothing... Nothing more bizarre... Then...

Societies that would purposely... willfully and consciously
Religiously and blissfully
Loudly and mercilessly

Form ranks on opposite sides of beliefs
And properly kill their very image... On the other bank.

*Far-off world of the future when generations will study humanity's history and be told of this particularity of our past: The earth had known for centuries wars that produced 'war heroes' that seemed to be worthy of special admiration. Having abolished 'organized' killing of any sort, the students would henceforth have to examine this piece of human history on the same basis as the roaming of dinosaurs at the dawn of time.*

## Reality and Worse

No illusions here. No cuddling needed.
No parental-pillow softness at bedtime readings.

No extraneous words to chase off monsters.
No stifling hugs from oversized grandparents,
Or summers evenings on cooling verandas under shy stars.

Tall tells of bearded uncles on tropical islands,
Late night scandals of eloping curvaceous cousins.

None or any of those idealized moments of midnight snacks had ex-
isted
Among the hospital-white ceramic and metallic sterility
Of the promiscuous sleeping quarters.

And worse yet... None would have.

*Upon locating his siblings who had remained with the parents, an 'orphan' is told that ironically he was the "fortunate one" to be institutionalized and raised in an orphanage.*

# Rambo Usurped

Rather like a confused captured soldier,
Dragged from the jungle mud and paraded past a collaborating audience:

A simplistic and simplified moral tale of re-telling.
Wild-eyed Hollywood plasticity of ethics.
Slight of hand to divert attention.

National metaphor of virility and strength,
Hawking adulterated, mythical bromide
To wash away the stony realities of history.

Jaded exhibitionism of varied technics of killing,
On a de-humanized one-dimensional enemy.

Mindlessly quieting the apocalyptic flow of guilt
Perpetrated by liquid Napalm.

Poetic irony... how the mechanized weight of revisionism
Cannot smooth the gentle letters of those names on the wall.

*The complicated, somehow sympathetic image of the original protagonist: A Viet Nam veteran, who is emotionally wounded, abandoned and misunderstood upon his return home. Versus the simplistic, cartoonish persona that John Rambo came to personify. In particular the pathos in the scene between Rambo and the mother of his African-American war comrade who had succumbed to the chemical spraying of the dense jungle.*

# Between the Gladiator and the Civil Engineer *

On an early spring morning,
This early version of a Roman engineer
Gathered his precious tools at the top of a rocky outcrop
In the middle of crazed cicadas
And aromatic herbs.

He drew a sketch in charcoal
Of an elegantly tiered aqueduct.

The first concrete image... of further images
That would appear to him in his sleepless Provençal nights.

In town, that morning,
Had arrived word of grandiose events from the formidable Circus
Maximus:

Tales of chariot races
Opposing the greatest of greatest stables of the Empire.

---

Followed, the quiet accomplishment of one:
And generations of drinking water.

For the other... Primordial screams and lost wagers.

* With much poetic license about and around the Pont du Gard in Nimes, France.

Reaction to newspaper articles and then commentary criticizing multi-million dollar contracts for sport figures and the underappreciated worth of a surgeon who had saved a person's life: "How many fannies does the surgeon put in the stands?"

## God Invented Love and Satan Jealousy

He is the one who tells you to look into her eyes
Discovering anonymous shadows

He is the one making you doubt a word's inflexion
The embrace in a hallway. A collegial kiss
An absence of presence
The intent under its wrapping

He is the one sleeping, making others toss
Dirtying deeds and oaths

He is the one who lives among the intimacy of scented letters
and the salt of tears

The iconic steamy hours sought in the pages of novels
Producing guilt admits moments of joy

Making culprits of all... Memories and sighs of abandon

## Dieu inventa l'amour et Satan la jalousie

C'est lui qui nous dit de la regarder dans les yeux
Pour y deviner des ombres

C'est lui qui nous fait douter de l'inflexion d'un mot
Une accolade dans un couloir. Un baiser amical

L'absence d'une présence
La raison d'être sous l'emballage

Celui qui dort au prix de l'insomnie des autres
Souillant les actes et les serments

C'est celui qui vit parmi l'intimité des billets parfumés
et le sel des larmes

La chaleur que l'on cherche dans les pages romanesques
Produisant le péché au sein du bonheur

Les rendant tous coupables... Souvenirs et soupirs

## Kafka's World
The Internet of Everything

*"In the deep future, we will go to sleep in world where even our dreams will be susceptible to scrutinizing for whatever purpose and evaluation." [Unattributed]*

World of unrestricted self-flagellation.
A universe of uncontrollable, self-induced guilt.
Digitized, multi-denominational big-brother confessionals.

Nothing ever done will be unknowable.
All of us, probably guilty of something, somewhere, somehow.

Your experiments with your favorite aunt's lipstick.
The carnal intimacies in your favorite hiding place.
That critical calculus grade.

An imposed fraternity of voyeurs,
Hidden in a religious fog of voyeurism.

"1984" and "Fahrenheit 451" in incestuous nuptials of forces.
Thus asphyxiating within and without.

The magnanimous and endless hopelessness
Of stifling connected perfection, as it were.

Our kind will be our own inquisitors:
Collaborationists in each corner of our daily lives.

Father confessors looking for sinners-in-soul,
In accidental passers-by.

---

Like the quaint and laughable escapism
Of scary B-movies of plastic background fame,
We will be facing the lasting solidity of a Hell of our own making.

Which unlike the atomic-bomb born Godzilla,
With unavoidable infectious diseases and maliciously crazed scientists,

Will not be pushed back into its bottle.

Gone the romanticism of our flesh and mind in chosen solitude.
Obliterated the difference between
Private...Public... Now... And then...

Our stolen first kiss, on that isolated first date,
Will live instead as an eternal closed-loop, YouTube infection.

*In the Brave New World of meta-information gathering by unimaginably big digital
storage, it will come to past that we will eventually be found guilty of having willingly
given up our privacy in favor of the interconnected attractions of the digitized world.*

## No Tombstone

Cross fertilization of thoughts.
Cross currents of ideas and images,

When iconic pieces of history
Find haunting reciprocal echoes against the other.

Fortuitous re-reading and reading into
Events and people that construct our past:

Offending the gods.
Rebutting the order of things.
Willfully consenting to do the unimaginable.

To be a good sister. A niece.
To be a good soldier.

To go thereafter
Eaten by doubts or supported by unwavering conviction.
Faulting the gods or our leaders.
Transgressing through pride.
Or allowing our humanism to be guided by it.

Lives lived. Destroyed or enhanced
By regal whims or executive choices.

But again and always this classical bare stage, nude to its essentials:

Action or inaction.

Humanity still and continuously gazing upon limits.
Guidance. Transgression or punishment.

And omnipresent throughout... the magnificence of triggers
That define central characters:
The stern simplicity of an edict, a coded message.

---

Still... One wonders what prompted the good captain
His self-imposed refusal of a tombstone:

Was it peace of mind for him or for others?

Strange this self-imposed eternal restless walk into eternity...

*Confluence of a re-reading of Antigone (by Sophocles and Anouilh) and an article on Captain Tibbett's (of Hiroshima fame) and the mention that the latter had refused a tombstone.*

# Insignificance

*"Man is equally incapable of seeing the nothingness from which he emerges and the infinity in which he is engulfed." Blaise Pascal [Pensées, 1670]*

The stuff of quirky-fun arcade along a quirky beach.
The stuff of teenage rituals of everlasting boyhood solidarity
And apparently eternal youthful memories.

Momentary illusions of bottomless perspectives,
Into the infinitely miniscule and meaninglessly small.

This face, looking into a face... seeing a trace of a smile
Regressing into insignificance.

Impatient remarks from impatient friends,
The smell of candy-cane spun into its pink puffed-up substance,

The cute arrogance of blinking circus-like colored electric bulbs,
Pretending to light the chill of the night.

Tripping over the wetness of invisible dew on the way back home
Giving calf muscles the solid feel of grounded purpose.

Strange...
How this disappearing smile on the brittle reflection of the mirrors
Now seemed like a declaration of some vague...
Bothersome truth... From the starry sky.

*Memories of looking into endless reflected mirror images facing each other at the local arcade in light of the results of the space telescope time-laps photographs of a dark section of space the size of the circumference of a pencil where thousands of galaxies were detected.*

# In Which God's Name?

A particular God's children?
Quite a feat to determine!

Since no one else would have the same sense of infallibility
In separating the good from the bad.

The Called from the Damned.

In a microcosm of disintegrated social structures,
Effaced traces of any possible human dignity,

Of the machinery of civilized time whose counter was reset to zero,
Of acrid smoke of burning flesh and ripples of blood in the greasy sand.

A village center akin to the hellish center of Dante's Inferno

Miserable humanity
With not a hint of its civil status.
Not an identification to relate to its position in the outside world.

Lightning fast entry among the miserable huts:
And then... What must be the intervention
Of some quasi-divine operation of some demented holy spirit,

Spawn from some creed... Some place... Some dimension.

Know-nothing illiterate gangs apparently able to decipher
In seconds... The complex entanglements
Of scriptures... Icons... Sacred texts and rituals,

As they chop heads and limbs:

Having determined to their absolute satisfaction,
Which gods resided in which respective hearts.


*Question in viewer's mind upon watching newscast about attackers coming into an
isolated African village full of the emptiness of civil war desolation and they can tell
who is of which religion?*

## "Fresh, Happy and Short"

*Homage to Arthur Rimbaud*

Contingence of illusion and reality.
Of matter and anti-matter.

Of adjectives ripped from the bowels of Dadaesque Hell.
Of jaded escapism into the contradictions of vaporous solidity.

Echoes of the nonsensical genesis of the movement,
Haphazardly chosen in haphazardly opened books.

Not unlike this benign symbol of a child's wooden horse,
Along with the pleasant imageries of war
So nonchalantly expressed on crowded sidewalk cafés

Perfect associative senselessness
Bloated verbal newspaper headlines

Perfect smoke screens
For the bloated soldiers' corpses to come.

All of it...
The prophetic exercise for the antonymous results
In a rotten... mournful... and endlessly muddy universe.

*In the month of August 1914, the European people go to war, which they imagine as not only "fresh and joyous" but also short: everyone is convinced of their return home before the turning of the fall leaves.*

*Au mois d'août 1914, les peuples européens partent pour une guerre qu'ils imaginent non seulement " fraîche et joyeuse ", mais courte : tout le monde est persuadé de pouvoir être de retour au foyer " avant la chute des premières feuilles " ( France-Amérique magazine of janvier, 2014 )*

## More Real in His Dreams

There was a surprising ease
In his repeated attempts to embrace her

The reach was somehow realistic,
The smile inviting.
                    The setting properly accommodating

Time... And apparently by their absence,
The laws of God and men, had not yet been invented in order to interfere.

The clutter and noise of things practical and ugly,
Gently wrapped in layers of the cotton
Of dispensation,
        Forgetfulness
                And happiness.

A nuptial perfume invaded his nostrils,
As he took deeper breaths to make her invade his very body:

So much so... That her presence dissolved in front of his confused eyes
... Waking up in the humid reality of sweat on his pillow.

*The artist to his Muse: "You live in my fiction"*

## Advertising Universe

Outer-worldly figure out of the glossy pages of Mythology.
Fear and awe, producing images
Of things and forces beyond the control of mere humans.

Like Ulysses and his men,
Running the Mediterranean gauntlets
Of dangerous and enticing sounds and visions.

Voices from above, speaking seriously to mankind passing by...

Such as the Marlboro man did in Times Square,
Blowing and puffing his cloud of ethereal message,

Like some wild beasts found in children's fables,
Generating irrational needs and wants
With crayons and shapes.

The men and women below had traded their cotton togas
For smart suits and high heels,

But the divinities, high on Olympus,
Are still trying to pull the strings of illusions on the villagers.

*Watching the universe of mirrors of Madison Avenue advertising in the situation comedy such as reruns of "Bewitched" and in the later series "Mad Men." Talented people cowering, elbowing and or using their energy to convince consumers to want products, any products, some of which not for their own or society's better good.*

## Real Obscenity [reprise 2014]

The horror... The unqualified horror!
Sinuous entanglement of flesh

Perceived carnal satisfaction and satiation
Of all sorts from all sources

Understood banishment from any possible redemption
Gladly accepted and willingly suffered,

For these...
The images a highly cultured quirk of civilized behavior

These...
The momentary celluloid returns
To unabashed basic hedonism strangely unknown
Even to our animal ancestors

Examples of which adorned
The form and substance of exquisitely fine mosaics
Of pinkish marble scenes hidden in the ashes of Pompeii

All of it seen and passively understood
By our various amused gods watching their progeny
Playing with their free will

These same tearful gods
In front of his ashes in Auschwitz

*Reflection on the life and death of Bernard Natan known as one of the earliest film
makers of sexually explicit films in France. No matter one's stand on people freely
fornicating in front of a camera, the proper use of obscene should be reserved for the
police apparatus that turned this Jewish man over to the Gestapo.*

# A Thousand Feet Underground

Impeccable marble sheen
Reflecting professional seriousness of stainless steel
Properly accented nuances of earth tone colors of cabinetry.

Dreamy softness of lighting,
Giving cocoon setting,

To this...
The idealized apogee of betterment of civilizations and cultures.

Indeed the best of best of worlds,
Since its meager riverside start,
On the primordial muds and smoking village fire:

Women preparing blacken flesh of local game.

This striking blond as the iconic descendant
Of earlier rituals of mankind:

The gestures, the colors and the smells have been kept
And welcomed.

Except for that hardened piece of conscience on her finger
Acting the part of a Greek chorus

*Mesmerized by the enormous diamond ring of a media-star cook as she whips some recipe and yet, this nagging thought about the South African mine worker looking at it for the first time.*

# Well... It's Still Sad... That's All

*"And the sea erases in the sand,*
*The foot prints of lovers gone by"*
Jacques Prévert

Yes, it still had a gentle tone.
There still remained in her voice the moistness of sighs.
She was saying what one must say when time decides for us,
And the heart accepts its defeat.

"I would have wanted... if only...
I don't want to... you know...
But...It's sad nevertheless."

## Enfin… c'est triste… c'est tout

« Et la mer efface sur le sable,
Les pas des amants désunis »
Jacques Prévert


Oui, la douceur y était toujours.
Il existait toujours dans sa voix l'humidité des soupirs.
Elle disait ce que l'on doit dire quand le temps décide pour nous,
Et le cœur accepte sa défaite

« J'aurais voulu… si seulement…
Je ne veux pas… tu sais…
Mais… c'est triste tout de même »

# The Color of Your Jacket

*A day at the ballpark*

Sleepy post week-end sociology course:
Dutifully taking down notes describing obscur tribal traditions
Of necklaces made of identifying trinkets.

Very serious beliefs...
In the very distant past
In different obscure parts of the globe
In obscur pastoral greenness.

Smart ancestors determining who "us" is and who "them" are,
Coming down the zigzagging path into their villages and lives

Detailed notations on mankind's attempts
In the life or death pursuit in uncertain settings.

_____

Did this modern-day father know that the stadium and soccer match
Had evolved into the place and purpose

For a free-fire zone in the contemporary fantasy world
Of imaginary fatal lines... Between us and them?

*Sport fan unaware that his favorite jacket would get him killed.*

## Love and Self-Worth

*Il était beau comme un soupir\**

He had the beauty of a sigh.*
The reserve of a whisper.
His voice, the undertones of early misty sunlight.

His glance became the golden cage of my soul
With the natural ease of the closing of his eyelashes
Upon the vibrating reflections off la Baie des anges

... his perfumed flesh invading my being....
And yet... Not possess it.

Time would languishly respond to his intimacies
With a magnanimous vanquished acquiescence.

Sweet like a May sunbeam
His perfumed flesh would invade my being...
And yet... Not possess it.

*Inspired by great moments of a woman's love when her integrity and standing does not allow her any expression of her feelings but instead lets her imagination take flight.*

## Semi-Virginal

The intensity of their relationship had engendered
Such primordial heat, such elemental energy,

That floating impurities of their previous carnal experiences
Had been incinerated.

Previous intimate knowledge of any and all others,
Existentially cleansed.

Making them gaze... and conjointly enter...
The emotionally virginal, natural landscape,
As nature had intended it to be.

Hence the reciprocal, gentle kiss upon each other's lips:

Stopping the whispered confessional flows
Of incestuously mingled,
Very earthy sighs.

Allowing lovers the mythological power of divinities:
That...Of creating in their lover...
Souls at their inception.

*"Do you want to know her first name?"*

## Demi-Vierge

La flamme de leur amour avait créé une telle chaleur primordiale,
Une telle énergie élémentaire,

Que les impuretés flottantes de leurs précédentes aventures
Avaient été incinérées.

Ces précédents moments d'intimité avec tout autre,
Existentiellement blanchis.

Leurs regards s'entrecroisant, ils entrent ensemble
Dans ce lieu émotionnellement vierge et naturel
Comme la Nature l'avait commandé.

Et cela…
Suivant un baiser réciproque sur les lèvres
Qui arrête l'aveu religieusement murmuré
Venant de soupirs très humains,
Fusionnant incestueusement.

Donnant aux amoureux le pouvoir des divinités :
Celui de faire de l'être adoré, comme elle l'était à sa création,
Une âme pure.

*« Tu veux que je te dise son prénom ? »*

# IV

# IN THE TRUE
# GARDEN OF EDEN

# In the True Garden of Eden

Like a Central African tribe of the past
With no words for snow:

No declination
Of the various solidities from the sky,

No differentiations and relationships
Of cold and its human effects.

Like a native Artic family:
With no fear of heat.

No tactile memory
Of warm sands and revealing bikinis.

One, with no association of snowy slopes
With skiing.

The other,
With no interest in beach volley-ball.

What if…
In its opinion of things in its own universe,
Nature…
Had no other judgmental option
But to impose, on moments of passionate embrace,

A complete unconditional absolution:
As a result of their genesis in divine happiness?

*"… I try to make nudity feel like a costume… " by the actress Adèle Exarchopoulos
of the sensual theme in the movie "Blue is the Warmest Color." This comment brings
to mind the iconic scenes showing Adam and Eve ashamed of their nakedness upon
leaving Paradise..*

## The Deer Hunter [redux]

Was it the very splendor in this animal
That spoke to him of human arrogance,
Found in their reciprocal glances?

The unmistakable awareness
Between the pulsating now and oblivion?

Without the examples of Greek tragedies,
Or the great classics of early morning college classes,

Had he learned in his steel hardened soul
The priceless, fragile value
Of the sparkle of sunlight on unblinking eyes?

*The Robert Di Nero character in "The Deer hunter" looking into his rifle telescope and not being able to shoot the beautiful, arrogant figure of the fully crowned male deer.*

## Force Majeure

The training was flawless. The indoctrination superb.
The weapons cutting-age
The adrenaline pumping.

The reptilian brain in charge and the frontal lobes on power saving.
The target obliviously nonchalant in the cross-hairs
The ground topography matching peacefully the aerial photographs.
The color of the tank the advertised despised hue.
The uniform the correct adversary-style.

And...
The slumping form
The exploding industrial neighborhood
The proper language of the screaming emanating from the tank
The color of the blood blending with the hated chest-icons

---

Left is a lump of ambivalence in the throat
Of the sniper
The pilot
The infantryman

Sending each one of them home to ponder
During a lull in the early evening warmth of a Babe Ruth game

About the wisdom of that little voice
According to which...

We all die a little individually
When we find big enough reasons
To do collectively what that small boy knew to be wrong.

*Basic training: "How to kill the enemy."*

# Divine Inspiration

A universe full of inspirational voices.

Imparted thoughts...
From star lights. Glowing bushes.
Magic springs. Telling stigmata.

Chicken entrails. Milky astrological globes.
Boudoirs séances full of coffee grounds,

Made of unequivocally directed futures.

Divine guides calling to action, with various degrees
Of human miseries, battles, maiming or shunning.

Turning, drinking friendly,
A tart chardonnay
Is indeed more on the human scale.

*At least Canon Félix Kir the priest who added current liquor to the tart Aligoté white
Burgundy wine did not have to invade any territories to spread his drink*

# Refusal

And thus Abraham refused the knife and opted for life

What if he had seen the reflection of the morning sun
On the unsheathed blade?

What if it had reminded him of the sparkle in his son's glance,
In the spring morning:
On his way to the hill and the flock of sheep?

What if the supple locks on the boy's nape
Reminded him that he was the living flesh of his living flesh...

And that it grounded his place, if temporarily, in Things?

What if the obedience of his son had made him understand
The momentary power given momentarily to a mere human...

To do momentarily good or evil?

And that the only tool... feeble as it was...
Was the will to push back death if only for that instant...

And allow for his son the momentary joy of earthly joys?

What if...
With all these whirling thoughts going through his whirling mind...
He stood up to his vaporous God...

And gave a concrete answer
Full of the only good that he knew:

That of a human joy...
Such as holding in his arms his living son...
Next to his beating heart?


*A personal reinterpretation of events on a rocky outcrop in the biblical past between God and Abraham: Seeing in this latter an "Homme révolté" in the manner of Camus: Thus acquiring his and our freedom from religious dogma by this refusal. Or possibly like a Prometheus daring to confront the gods to allow for a measure of autonomously driven happiness for our kind.*

## Divine Conflict

Still waiting for Godot
Thus... God rested...
The intricacies of the Universe behind,
Galaxy-wide equations of gravitational laws solved,
Untold number of civilizations and settings in place,

Cleverly revealed pieces of his own existence,
Theologically absorbed... Through cleverly intertwined protocols
Of mythologies in various stages of revelatory dreams:

God had left behind
A fully equipped kitchen
With all the required cook books,
All the listed ingredients available for easy use... if you will..

---

Yet... And again:

This God-wrenching tearful prayer,
From this nineteen-year old... From third street in Brooklyn...

... Wanting to see his mother again!

*Thoughts provoked by Army chaplain in news clip giving invocation for fresh-faced*
*Second World War soldiers about to land in Normandie*

# Cinéma Vérité

*To Docteur Drieux, his splendid humanity and gloriously fatalistic fight against the Plague*

Beautiful lives: suckling to bloated breasts.
Eye of camera unemotionally capturing
Cinéma-vérité setting of immemorial maternal caring

Miniature fingers
Seeming to wave their appreciation.

Miniature eyes
Fixated on this magnificent figure,
Looking down with the shadow of a smile.

Mythological instant. Iconic stature.
Microcosm of the enormity of acting.

Trying to dilute, swallow by warm swallow,
The liquid of pure Evil.

*Reaction to Journal Afrique of December 4, 2013 showing mothers breast-feeding their babies conceived by rapes*

# Fertility Rite

Stiff-necked executives at the asymptotes of disco poses,
Allowing glimpses of expensive time pieces.

Chanel-scented lace spouses in silk evening dresses
With dangerously unguarded hints of rounded forms.

Impeccable manners and endless introductions
With intrusive hints of office protocol.

Memorized C.Vs and proper body separation for small talk.
Shameless positioning for networking.

Bland understated opinions and properly repressed laughter,
Followed by non-metered ingestion of overpriced wine.

---

Loosening of bow-tie.
Abandon of high heels and restraints.

Explosion on the floor of images of social rites of passage.
Tribal fertility spirits taking over bourgeois-class bodies.

Spirits of abandonment and hedonism,
Producing hip-humping gyrations
Floating in pre-nuptial vapors.

*Observing the subtle yet recognizable undercurrent of primordial sexual energy on a dance floor at a very high end marriage: Mostly executive level guests in modern very glitzy hotel setting. Women, with silky dresses, pulsating their hips to the Big Bang echoes of the bass guitar.*

## Last Words

The authors of religions
Have had their enemy properly in their sight from the beginning.

Single-mindedly
Pointing an accusing human finger
At the unvanquished enemies of mankind:

The impossible... Santa Claus... the moon.
Striving for pieces of absolute dispersed in semantics

While for some artists...
In their apportioned corner of things
Quietly knowing the laws of the end-game,

Destiny will be a reflection in the mirror of their art
Appearing in the consciousness of the Other

———————————————————————

Such as the vibrant spirit of the composer still living
In the solidarity of the extra heartbeats of the lovelorn musician
In the orchestra seats

*"I knew for the first time that there was beauty in the world."*
*From the young Inspector Morse character (Endeavour) to his heroine the opera diva.*
*Spectacular observation on the **sublime divide between art and reality** and how art*
*can alter the latter: because in spite of her life altering impact on Endeavour, through*
*her angelic voice, the singer is after all a cold blooded killer.*

# Between Notre Dame de Paris and a Vieux Calvados

*Searching for some stability*

Standing as backdrop during sleepless bistro nights
through the acrid smoke of Gitanes,

Were these arches the possible antidotes
To the bland boredom of totalitarian esthetics and ethics?

Vaccines against the dusty gray cement uniformity
Of uninspired Stalinism?

Forgiving the inquisitional similarities
Of all the unbending dogmas?

Any dogmas?
Biblical or political?

Was it revisionism for the eyes?
Architectural doctrinal heresy?

Like all grandames, she stood for the solidity of conviction:
The key-stoned edifice of human visions.

Any vision:
Of this world or possibly none at all.

The slenderness of its Hugoesque buttresses
Giving momentary refuge for some benign stability.

Any stability:
Till the end of Time or of this drink.

In the image of the universe of this sidewalk café
Peopled by a gentle summer crowd
Searching for symbols of momentary belief:

Any belief:
Real or otherwise.


*Philosophical conversation, in the Paris of the 1970's, with hardline French Communists
and Atheists who had a refreshingly uncomplicated and unapologetic reverence for
Notre Dame de Paris*

# Channeling Charles Aznavour

Generously violated
Strangely spiritually naked like Grecian marble
Bleached by the probing sensitivity

Incapably captive
Of our susceptibility to his gaze into the recesses of our soul

Daring to tell all others
That which we muffle into the pillow's folds

Metamorphosis of our perspective
Into the fertile soil of emotional Androgyny

Putting us in the embrace of our embrace
Reflecting our whispers back to us

Speaking on our behalf with glorious ease
In the interpretive immortal codes of the human inenarrable

*Inspired by the intrusive feeling that this artist seems to penetrate the lives of his listeners.*

## Detention Camps and Chocolate

Outside of the Canons of ethics
On the wide margins of decency

In the dark corners of children's nightmares
In a universe of dead Santa Claus and perverted Tooth Fairy

Have been built worlds of Kafkaesque dimensions
With Rules of Dadaesque splendor

A world of such breathless Existentialist corruption
That it shames even the righteous act...

Making the sunrise blush upon its awareness
Of giving warmth to such as us

*Inspired by NPR interview of David Lasken author of* The Family *where he describes Jewish children dying in front of horrified GI's after ingesting chocolate bars from their would-be saviors.*

## Into the Woods and Beyond...

What was not to like…
Late at night and the perfumed smells of the evening on him.

Late fall midnight-drive back to the university dorm.
Silhouetted cow herds in moonbeam.

"You know what...
I'll open the window of the Volkswagen
And turn up the radio."

What Victor Hugo would call a "Nuptial night:"
Generating thoughts of more.

Cheap Portuguese wine,
As proper metaphor to counterbalance penny-less Junior-year
Filled with the sweet curiosity of blind dates.

Memorized intricacies of this 'cow' road
And hypnotic découpage of tree tops against full moon.

Life and the car, seem to float
In the vigor of the magic of youth.

And then...
"The sharp left turn! ... The sharp left turn!

*At the end of a holiday family meal, surrounded with his family and holding a Cognac snifter, a man reflects on an event from his university days: "This would have killed my parents."*

# Pigeon

Splendidly gentle Stoicism
Grandiose microcosm of animal elegance

Trembling remnants of life's doomed dignity
Pushing back death

Un-verbalized statement of an iconic moment
Compliments of roadside theater of the Absurd

Rainbow sheen, from sparkling long feathers,
Rolling off like delusional armor against time

Lofty personal mythology invading once more
The muddy side of the highway

*Seemingly stoic dying pigeon standing by the side of a busy highway, waiting for the next moment. All with splendid stiffen attention and jerky neck movement.*

## Bring Your Own Dirt

Dutifully having brought his bagged lunch to his corner desk
Silently paid his motor vehicle taxes
Touchingly sent his mother's annual mother's card
Grumblingly recycled his newsprint
For forty-two years

Put up an increasingly decreasing Christmas tree
Sent an ever regressing amount to his children's birthdays
Bought a scandalously weaker virgin olive oil

Having made due of decrepitude from his appliances
And his body parts

Having been continuously cut off at the corner stop sign
Ignored one last time by beautifully clueless waitress

Could it have come as anything other than poetic surprise
To suffer one more imposition?

*Forced into thinking about the details accompanying one's funeral while impatiently
following an overloaded little pick-up truck that eventually turned into a local cemetery
to a waiting crew of undertakers: It was evidently carrying the needed loose dirt for
the ceremony*

## *La Princesse de Clèves* [redux]


There was something painterly about her presence:
The clair-obscur of the coffee shop chiseling the contours of her face.

A subdued smile appeared...
No... More like a Hellenistic pout.

The moment was akin to noble exhausted warriors,
Admitting defeat, after the nobility of the effort.

It...
Had to end.

It is true what literature says about the human heart...
Theirs were indeed breaking.

All the extraneous strings,
All the subtle wavelets made of deepening wrinkles and longer
reciprocal distances,
All the fading memories trying their best at plugging temporal leaks,

The Darwinian logic of cold realities,
The spin of centrifugal forces pulling them apart,

All forming a tormented mass of remaining ethical embers in his
soul...

... Thus whispering upon leaving her embrace:

"I have never imposed myself... I will not now."


*Inspired by the generosity of sentiments of self-abnegation as exemplified in* La
Princesse de Clèves *the seventeenth century French novel by Madame de La Fayette.*

## La Princesse de Clèves [redux]

Il y avait quelque chose du tableau de maître en la voyant :
Le clair-obscur du café ciselait le blanc de ses joues.

Un sourire plein de réserve apparut...
Non... Plutôt une sorte de moue Hellénistique.

Le moment rappelait ces guerriers nobles exténués
Acceptant leur défaite après la noblesse de l'effort.

Tout cela…
Devait finir.

La littérature dit de vraies choses du cœur humain…
Le leur, en effet se brisait.

Toutes ces ficelles qui les retenaient inutilement
Tous ces sillons formant des rides grandissantes et une distance entre
eux réciproquement plus longue.

Tous ces souvenirs s'effaçant qui tentaient  de leur mieux de calfeutrer
les fuites,
Toutes les forces d'attraction centrifuge les repoussant l'un de l'autre
Toute cette logique darwinienne faite de froides réalités,

Réussirent à rallumer chez lui les quelques derniers tisons d'intégrité
Qui lui firent murmurer, alors qu'il quittait ses bras :

« Je ne me suis jamais imposé… Je ne le ferai pas maintenant. »

*Inspiré par la générosité des sentiments exemplifiée dans* La Princesse de Clèves,
*roman du dix-septième siècle de Madame de La Fayette.*

# Same Time Next Year at the Fontaine Saint-Michel

Couscous still cheap...
Blinking multicolored bulbs still leading
To menus from North Africa and obscure landlocked Asian states.

The street, people and pigeons
Still not recognizing time or languages

The boulevard
Typically difficult to navigate during students strikes.

Gitanes and Gauloises,
The preferred perfumes du jour.

An endless energy on the side walk cafés:
With no lack of topics. No lack of problems to resolve.
No Eldorados too far to reach by hitch-hiking.

No lack of incomprehensible philosophies,
Revolutionary teaching technics or research matter:

Too vaporous to analyze, too dangerous to critique
Or too sacred to destroy...

_____

...But it was during those golden hours of renewal
When walking... In opposite directions on the Boul'mich,
That they would lock glances through the insane proliferation of traffic

...That time... had seemingly stood still
Having chosen rather to wait for their return in each other's embrace.

Until this moment of silence
Under the cotton sheets of an atypical prudishness covering their
nakedness,
In the mannerism of post paradisiac museum scenes

When he inevitably felt jealous
Toward that specific time... that specific space
That had filled and fulfilled her.

Toward those very seconds, those minutes... hours and days
That had had the privilege of acting the role of her daily debris.


*Based on the theme of the play and movie "Same time next year"*

.

# Totems of Desire

*Laisse-moi devenir / Allow me to become*
*L'ombre de ton ombre / The shadow of your shadow*
*L'ombre de ta main / The shadow of your hand*
*L'ombre de ton chien / The shadow of your dog*
*"Ne me quitte pas," Jacques Brel*

Could it be that on this side of Merlin?
On this side of Celtic smoky grottos.

Of galactic parallel worlds
Incestuously exploding into one another.

On the other side of moral codes.

Could it be that the magic of incantations?
The power of passionate formulas.

Could it be that from simple carnal genesis?

The loving purity.
The transparently pure longing of lovers.

Could it be,
In this new world of unlimited possibilities,

That the very humility of certain totems of the universe,

Lead to the immediacy... to the translucence of sheer cotton
Over the willing flesh of desire?

*Envying the totems that routinely touch the person we love.*

# Totems du Désir

*Laisse-moi devenir*
*L'ombre de ton ombre*
*L'ombre de ta main*
*L'ombre de ton chien*
*"Ne me quitte pas," Jacques Brel*

Serait-il possible que de ce côté de Merlin ?
De ce côté des grottes enfumées Celtes.

Des mondes galactiques parallèles
Explosant incestueusement l'un dans l'autre.

De l'autre côté des codes de la moralité.

Serait-il possible que la magie des incantations?
La force des formules passionnées.

Serait-il possible qu'à partir de simples genèses charnelles ?

La pureté amoureuse.
La pureté transparente du désir des amants.

Serait-il possible
Dans ce nouveau monde des possibilités sans limites ?

L'humilité même de certains totems de l'univers

Amènerait à la proximité... à la transparence du coton fin
Couvrant la chair disponible du désir ?

*L'envie envers les totems qui touchent quotidiennement la personne que l'on aime.*

# EPILOGUE

# ARTIST IN A
# PIXELATED WORLD

# The Artist and the Muse

*Homage to Alfred de Musset: "La nuit de mai"*

One of the driving energy in Alfred de Musset's poetry is his tumultuous relationship with George Sand (Amantine-Lucie-Aurore Dupin). She was a tortuously complicated figure in his life and a powerful muse for some his art. In "Nuit de mai," in particular, the lonely poet is in the middle of the night hoping for inspiration to come back.

In this series of conversational reflections, inspired by Musset's lyricism, I envision the poet, the muse and a chorus, in this conversational frame, driven by the creative process.

Some of the themes and verses for this epilogue have been opted or adapted from portions of my previous poems. Here, I take the opportunity to revisit, in a different format, some of my marginal notes made when working originally on these various poems. It allows me to pursue my ideas [in an "Ars poetica" fashion] of the place, purpose and interconnectivity between art and reality, the inspirational imagery and the poem: Topics of particular importance, as they are through much of my poetry, such as the apparent contradictions in what can be used as ingredients of poetry. I am referring, once again, to the tension between reality and art; the solid and the vaporous: as exemplified by the choice of this specific opening quote by Victor Hugo's on the title pages and my particular use of the Delacroix painting on the cover.

# I

## Untouchable

*In homage of the "Girl with the Pearl Earring" (by Johannes Vermeer)*

The poet
You are my only link to the temporal limits of love.
You live where mere men can only survive for an instant.

It is a rarefied world of the impossible:
A place of inhuman choices,
Found between the lines of literature.

Inhuman, because... like you... not of this world.

It is the place chosen by the playwright
With a drab and dead personal life,
Who presents to us, between stage right and left,

Remembrances of you... in breathless moments of fervor.

You were there,
When crippled and half-blind painters remembered...
Like yesterday,
The shivering warmth of pink feminine flesh,
Under the impressionistic shade of poplars trees.

You were there,
When sickly, drug addicted... abandoned writers,
Now alone in their seventh floor, Parisian alcove,

Described their most beautiful poetic moments of life:
The perfume she wore... the way her eyes closed upon a kiss.

---

You are made of pieces of the unreal:
Phantoms left in the corners of my mind
Where I reconstruct translucent visions of happiness on earth.

You are no less than the incandescence of love:

In the loving glance of the being that one loves.

---

You make it possible to know...
To know, as surely as any mortal knows,
That upon my awakening,
You will still be asleep next to me.

---

You will reconstruct for me...
The too often neglected banality of evening joys
While shopping at six o'clock at the corner grocery store..

Only to wake me up… my fingers still on the keys of the machine,
In the mud of reality…And, you... gone.

The muse
I will be with you, when you wake up, a mere man,
With all your weaknesses… all your cowardice.

Forced to choose.
To choose… on one side of life…
Between the stability of the daily routine,

The invading decrepitude,
The solidity of the noise of people passing in the street,

And… on the other side,
The refreshing, but vaporous clouds
…of the impossible…of the untouchable,

---

Of a glance…of THIS glance.

You will be back in a place surrounded by solidity,
Where happiness can so easily become no more than a fantasy:
Something to which we have no... Or no longer any right.

And you will force yourself to write or paint again,
Things... that do not... or no longer exist:

If not in your heart… And on the canvas of a museum,
A sheet of music or words on a page,

In front of which one passes…one hears... one reads,
With envy, holding one's breath,
Wanting, in turn, to have known the source for this inspiration:

Now the spouse of the eternal.

# II

## Untouchable
*Sculpture of a nude*

The muse
I live away from the carnal... in the forbidden space,
Between embrace and need.

I wear the aura of the Madonna,
Found under the transepts of churches.

I am made of the beautiful pink marble,
From the burning hills of the Mediterranean.

And until you came... I had known
Only the inert mineral warmth of stone.

You came and fashioned me in the fever of the moment,
And transformed me,
Making me malleable from the heat of your fervor.

Representing now, the plasticity of hidden desires,
Under the cotton of pleasure.

My veiled curves
Were cut into the hard marble of the temporal,

Precisely where it offered itself
To the intimacy of your chisel.
And... once the dust settled on your studio's floor,
Once the discreet sheet having fallen to my feet,
Once the workplace dark and empty,

I witnessed you... immobile and immobilized
In front of me... your creation.

I remained a vision of the warmth of happiness,
Softly petrified in the chaos of reality.

Chorus

She leaves the poet desperately searching
For a way to reclaim the Muse in his arms,

In order to reconstruct this woman, hiding behind the object.

The artist, now in his bed... eyes wide opened,
Tortured by dreams... made of mineral clouds.

# III

## Between Inspiration and the Void
## Poetry and Reality

The poet
I remember envying the gods:
And the inenarrable things they have created.

These gods who wrote in lightning bolts
Setting fires to the dead and dry twigs…
Of the silent and puritan savannas.

Setting pagan fires in our entrails…
Forcing us to create.

Oh!… To taste... Once more... in their natural abundance…
The children of the poisonous and biblical fruits of hedonism.

Morsels left behind by these same divinities
Thus keeping alive the flame of inspiration, preventing it from dying
from the winds of forgetfulness.

Gods who gave us a taste for the sensuality of sight
And the fear of losing it.

Gods who gave us the craving to tell
And the insidious fear of having nothing more to say.

Gods who put the object of desire in our arms
And its powdery disintegration on our fingers tips:

Leaving us with memories of precious objects
Dissolving in front of our eyes.

The obsessive need to write faster amidst the fear of losing the moment…
And... yet, the deadly sin of rote-writing.

---

And so… you left me... alone,

Trying to touch, once more, quasi-sensual fondling,
attempting to  reconstruct the past.

The gods gave me the taste for the eternal…
…and the evaporation of the moment

They are the ones who gave me my first taste
For the bitter awareness……the bitter awareness

That love alone……love in its complex purity…
…does not give to its lovers…
…the right to love… and this… forever.

———————————————————————

Full of their nonchalance, these same blasé gods
Gave me the taste of parted lips…

…and the horrible sensation of knowing that embrace is not timeless.
That the sweat soaked emanations of the present
Will face the blanched skeletons

Which will have lost the quivering of life.

It is then that we decide
To not venture any further in this desert of tomorrow.

———————————————————————

And so on blistered feet
I fall in the burning sand

Letting myself go into the darkness
Amidst the whiteness of the crystalline minerals.

Letting myself die… Facing the sun…
… Hearing… No… Listening…

Listening
To the rubbing the sand next to my ears sinking into the dune.

I hear the cries of a bird of prey…

…this is the last breath of a universe calling me back to life…

Leaving me in a strange ambivalence.

A multilayered ambivalence before my death…
Haunted with previous images of a precious meaningful life

Chorus
And so he dies… the way one falls into a stupor:
Disdainful of a world where…

…love alone…
…love in its complex simplicity…
…does not give to its lovers…
…the right to love… and this… forever.

It is then that just before entering eternal happiness…
…he awakens,
to the much... too common daily noises…
…everyday silt acting as background noise.

He wakes up in a universe
Guided by rules and morality,

To once again, recreate all this, in a world,
Where…even love,

Lives in the shadow of its own demise in time.

# IV

## Under the Reserve and the Passion

The poet
I had long wished and I had long suspected,
That Mythologies could at any moment invade my world of mortals.

That the world of literature
Could at any instant rise from the dull reality of a morning commute
And prove to be more real than my morning cup of coffee,

That, for no apparent reason,
I would turn to the left of my desk, one day,
And see you.

The muse
I didn't know if you could see me.
Recognize who I was

The poet
I knew who you were
By the cosmic silence that preceded you.

It was as though the room had been cut off from the world.
As though, if I had gone into the hallway
That I would have stepped into strangeness...

The muse
I wanted to guide you into the magic and majesty.
Of the rich confusion of the rites of passages

Moments that have so often prompted artists
Into the awareness of Time.

Thus wanting to extend it, continue it
And for the first time knowing the fear of losing it

The poet
I became your accomplice

And thus could see, on the walls of the cave,
The sacred images of the non-mortal world .

The muse
You had the right to enter:
You had the passion

The muse
The passion of rites of passage
Such as the ones
In the middle of a field of a New England winter

The poet
*(Dreamingly)*
It felt like warm sand.

The muse
I am the face of multiple realities and possibilities.

The poet
I had given up.
I had resigned myself to accepting illusions... as illusions
And that dreams would be followed by mornings
... Where you did not exist... and could not be touched.

The muse
You knew that I was there all the time.

The poet
I had to believe that you were not just the clever fabrication
Of disillusioned artists.

I always felt... I always knew,
When driving back to my dorm late that night,

That within the Big Bang background drone of Faustian temptations
Could still be heard the sound of her eyes lashes closing upon a kiss.

That among the common filth of stacks of invoices
... And Calvinistic duties...

That the beauty of the Devil was indeed
That He is still… beautiful…

The muse
*(Seamlessly continuing)*
And his embrace…
Doubly worth the eternal price he had always demanded.

That the beauty of dreams and envies can easily… too easily,
Impregnate susceptible ethics
And thus allow us to find what made the gods delineate some things
beyond some unapproachable limit.

The poet
*(Softly)*
Yes! Yes!

The muse
Like a Rembrandt's rendering of Bathsheba's gaze
As she sits on the threshold of what is human in her soul

The poet
*(Seamlessly)*
Curiosity. Lust and superb weakness.

The muse
Yes!
You do see all these contradictions in the souls of mortals?!

The poet
I have seen it through you.
Because of you.

---

You have kept me thirsty for more of you
By offering pieces of your magical soul,

In which I had detected the possibilities of hidden folds in your being.

Presences…

That were so basic to who you are.
Things and people that I have never dared to probe.

A presence or presences
That if in any way questioned...

Would have made you crumble in front of my very eyes:
An undercurrent of passion under a cloak of reserve.

The muse
I wanted to tell you but...

The poet
No! I have never wanted to impose myself on you
There is the fragility of the butterfly about you:
The thirst for independence and need of flight

Chorus
*(He stops and looks fondly upon her)*
He gazes into eyes of wilting moral ambivalence:
The one of a divinity with feet of clay.

The one of the splendidly virtuous Bathsheba
Who knows...that she will give herself to King David.

Such were his thoughts upon glancing over his right shoulder.
Upon a spell binding presence of richness and intonations.

The poet
She was a multiplicity of incarnations and reincarnations of symbols:
Intelligence… femininity… strength and fragility,
Glancing all at once upon me..

# V

## In Homage to Antoine de Saint Exupéry
## "Le Petit Prince"
*Flower of Paradise*
*Far away, in Hawaii, lives a garland of flowers*

The poet
On the warm side of my soul
You appeared as a flower...

The muse
I was thirsty for the warmth of Hawaiian breezes:
Protective hands and knowing tender caresses.

I had risked my life by entering the solidity of your world.
I only had the fragility of my petals to protect me
And the protective shadows in the recesses of my heart
To bare myself to you.

The poet
I turned my back to the sun,
I became lost in the splendor of your beauty.

All I wanted to do was to retain you...
... By and with my glance
I wanted to capture your presence
In the sunbeams and in Time.

Chorus
She had come into his life on the sun-bathed side of his soul:
Arriving under the appearance of a flower of Paradise.

The muse
You found me on a joyous wind
And in the freshness of things future.

---

I am the sap of youth, the humidity of life.

The poet
But I committed the sin of arrogance:

I confused your approachability to me
With dominance and sole possession.

I selfishly thought that you lived through my admiration.

The muse
You must know from your sleepless nights
That beauty must remain elusive to be worth its price.

I am... I exist... That is all.
This knowledge deep inside of you,
During tortuous sleepless nights, must suffice.

Chorus
It was done so for all your predecessors
And she must be there for you successors.

---

Your hold on her is only as powerful as your talent.

The poet
I would die for the inspiration of yesterday

Chorus
She also craves for nourishment
Her roots look for the solid richness in Things.

The poet
Is it why her stem is bending toward the soil?

*(In an alarming tone to the muse)*
You... you are dying in the shadow of my presence!

Chorus
As he moves away from her... one last time...
He sees her shimmering, up there, by herself
Learning that day,
Finally... and in his heart,
Full of the moist whispers of her name on his lips,
The price that is asked of true lovers.

# VI

## The Other Side of Her Life
*To George Sand*

The poet
You open doors that most mortals
Would rather keep closed.

The muse
Do you have faith in me?

The poet *[shyly]*
I must...
I have waited so long for this moment

But unlike Moses I cannot just be given a glance of the Promised Land
And accept to look away... to walk away.

You... you represent envies and truths that are dangerous,
By their privileged status in the universe.

You represent one of the rare realizable claims for mortal
To an eternal reserved for divinities.

You make it possible to rub our dry flesh
Against the moist amoral gratuitous.

The muse
Is this what you must possess?

The poet
You know perfectly well what you represent.
You have been there all the while.
At all my rites of passage.

At all these first times that made the moment doubly precious
By its ephemeral splendor.

The muse
I am aspirations, envy and dreams.
I am the impossible incarnation of fantasy and reality.


The poet
You are my inspiration, my envies and my dreams.
And you allow me to live in fantasy and reality.


The muse
I am the other side of the wall.
I am the vapors of your morning cup of coffee escaping out of the window.
I am the accidental glance across the train tracks
Upon a woman whose own eyes had been fixated on a hungry void.

---

*(Continuing)*
Does it scare you?


The poet
*(Slight pause but then resolutely)*
It does not scare me.


The muse
I will be your perfect canvas.
I will be the past, present and future... all in one improbable singularity.


I will be your trusted friend and obedient mistress.
I will know what you will know.


I have been waiting for you... But you know... you must know...
You must suspect, as an artist,
That it is the craving that drives you,


The sleepless night... the nuits blanches...
This very night,


Such things nourish me. Bring me to life.
I do not exist without you.

The poet
I suspected that on the days of blank pages,
Followed by my most precious writings.
The muse
Yes but...

The poet
But?

The muse
Think... think.
What is the single most frustrating.... Most powerful inspirational tool?

The poet

---

*[Looks into her eyes]*

---

The muse
What is it about me?

The poet
Oh! God!
You know about that?

The muse
I am your muse *[Gently.... Motherly...]*

The poet
You won't admit it to me then?

The muse
I cannot... This part of me is also what I am
I am that memorable moment in art
That reveals the unapproachability that the artist craves.

That fold of my soul... that if flattened....
Would represent the predictability of your trip to work in the morning.

The poet
But I must know all about the person with whom I share your heart.
What is more important,
I suspect that this person enriches you in your so special way.


The muse
You are correct
But that side of my life... after you... will be my refuge.
I will carry it in my heart


The poet
*(Raising his voice)*
For whom?


The muse
*(Gently smiling)*
Others should also have Paris after you.
You need envy... not fulfillment.
You cannot possess me... You were not meant to...


She kisses him on both cheeks

# VII

## Dream Sequence:
## The Painting

Cold artist studio. Silhouettes of easels standing like phantoms.
A cottony-light flitters through a prudish curtain on the wall.

The poet
In a nervous, breathless panic.
He practically rips the cloth aside

My vision of you has reappeared
I had kept you under the generic calm of a landscape

..... Trying to imprison and appease unspeakable passions
under layers of pretty watercolors
living in a sleepy two dimensional world.

Chorus
But, infinitesimal cracks have come to the surface of the paint
and into your mind.

Among the sedate prairie green of this landscape.
Are now escaping needles of light radiating like curtains in you studio:
This seemingly razor sharp brightness makes the darkness darker.

The poet
There is a self-sustaining energy here
That is melting the pigments of organic greens

And slowly, temptingly… like a burlesque stage
The landscape is giving way to the sinuous intensity of an internal
vision of a reclining nude.

Chorus
A milky carnality inundates all the corners of the room.

The poet
Your presence hurts my glance
From trying to capture you all at once:

He whispers:
Like the first time... Like the very first time

Full voice:
I remember reconstructing you from mere black shadings
of charcoal sketches

But your image inescapably seared my lonely soul:
My thoughts... eventually ending as thoughts of precise paint onto the
canvass.

Chorus
Picks up seamlessly the poet train of thought

Dreams of colors. Sighs and hues... in varied nuances of life.
Screams of vermilions streaked into lightest touches of pink.

All from burning memory...
late in the voids of insomnia.

The poet
Well before the paint had dried
I had to confess my sin of arrogance in front of the universe
Acting the role of my jury

I was only a mere intermediary... a mere conduit between worlds
My art had not claim to personal intimacy... to privacy:

Art transcends... it must.

I, then realized that you had not belonged to my eyes only
And that the instant that you had languorously leaned back
With your porcelain arms behind your head
With your thighs hinting at hidden happiness.
Within layers of flesh colored splendors....
... That you had escaped ownership.

That the pliability of those cherished folds were the beginning and end:
The place where things evaporate into carnal perfume.

The muse
I am the priceless Odalisque posing on the wrinkles of a poor
bohemian bed
I am the translucent Arabian magic,
The surprising greenish metallic sheen in the cotton fibers.

---

And we do not have the right to deny this joy to the Other
As you had tried to deny it to yourself for those many years.

Chorus
the way you ran your finger tips on the paint:
The way one would barely skim the lips of a sleepy satiated lover.

Feeling guilt in a fertile hazy state:
The one between bottomless sleep and frantic creativity.

The uncontrolled mind and body instinctively measuring
The eternal truth of Things:

The muse
Picking up the though seamlessly

Of the frustration of untouchable beauty.

Chorus
It is when… In a quasi-religious prise de conscience:
The poet sees the cowardice of his lack of belief in art
In his own art…

.

Taking down the remaining curtain:
And letting his passionate gaze rest… There…
Where all passions eventually and rightly should live…
In the perfumes of art.

# VIII

## The Fable of the Artist and His Muse
*Inspired by the relationship between George Sand and Alfred de Musset.*

Chorus
At home in the land of plenty
With friends who loved the sprint of his humor.

The poet
I would jump from misty imagery to the concrete:
From subtle sensuality, to the urban silt.

The muse
I inspired ideas as transparent as the finest black lingerie
To the blackest of political pronouncements.

The poet
Women caused me no fear
I would approach with them with greatest of ease.
Eyeing ingots of sparkling treasures,
Found in the 'quasi-foreplay-value' of the Genesis of friendship.

Chorus
Colleagues and acquaintances looked forward to his arrival:
From frivolous parties to stuffy family gatherings.

Knowing that he would insert himself
At different levels, into different levels of conversation.

The muse
But like many great souls
He was made of complex, brittle… complicated machinery.
Like a jeweled time piece.

Chorus
His… was a mind that was made to accommodate
Only one eventual sister soul… his Muse…

The muse
His... was a mind that was made to accommodate
Only one eventual sister soul... Me.

Chorus
She was made, by the magic of chance.
To his specifications.

He could only drink... he could only transcribe,
Things and visions emanating from this vaporous being
Who appeared, so believingly, in his childhood fairy tales.

The poet
And so I began the rest of my life:
Alone for the first and last time,

My hands on my chest
Trying to link the rhythm of my heart
To the waves on the lake where we had met.

Chorus
There were remains of streaks of spiritual tears
Shimmering in the blotches of decreasing sunlight.

Everyday… henceforth…
He would dress himself and his mind
For her inevitable reappearance,

While limpid water of other presences
Was trickling within his easy reach.

The poet
But having tasted the spectacular molecules
Of the vitality of creative life
I had lost a taste for the template of the mundane.

---

I am victim of the subtle mortal danger of the artist…
… That of coming across a spectacular Muse

With intricate, complicated sides.
Rich in topography and angles

Made of exact and exacting formulas:
Akin to the ones of Medieval alchemy.

All these details of her that magically, perfectly
Matched the gapping cavity in my heart:

Chorus
Miraculous geometric volumes,
Worthy of the science of Merlin,

That had, on a fateful day,
Found its perfect and perfected niche
In his soul and body.

The poet
Nothing and no one else could or would ever do.

Chorus
And so, he was dying… in full regalia,

The muse
With his crimson vest neatly buttoned to hide to the world
The place where I had lived.

# IX

## Forbidden Fruit
*Reflections on Lancelot and Guinevere*

The poet
It was the elegance, the tenderness of your rejection,
That kept me convinced to the very end
Of your worthiness of my love.

You are generous of heart and pure of mind

The muse
I was forced to set unwelcomed boundaries
To keep you from accidentally feel the fluttering of my knees.

Chorus
Semi platonic skimming of her face,
Met with the beginnings of puritanical reflexes.

Emotional survival, clarity of mores
Were taking charge of unregulated drives.

And whether in a cavernous frigid hall of a medieval castle,
Or separated by a stern stick shift overlooking a lake,

The gesture was historic and proper.
Repeated and repeatable.
Expected and respectful.
And eternally hurtful.

The poet
She had become... untouchable.

The muse
Thus, on the other side
Of what was your existential decision,
Existed what delineated your freedom of action...

... her legitimate claim to earthly happiness.

Chorus
That is where he learned,
That is when he knew,

That the luscious fruit, its fragrance,
Fleshy pulp and raspy taste,

Was as real and present
As was his remaining passion.

But would live henceforth
On separated sides of that reality.

# GLOSSARY

**Abraham**: Prophet and common denominator in Judaism, Christianity and Islam. The scene in the poem "Refusal" envisages the prophet as not agreeing to kill his son and thus radically change the course of history, societies and civilization.

**Absurdism**: Generally, the term describes a silent world with no absolutes and therefore no divine guidance. [See Existentialism]

**Africa**: General heading for many poems in this book in which I deal directly or peripherally with this continent, in particular Cinéma vérité that describes these violated women breast feeding their babies, the result of their rapes, in the D.R.G.[Démocratique République du Congo]. This theme is unfortunately a metaphor for the horrible, inhumane and indescribable savagery visited on this country, among others in the area.

**Antigone** [by Jean Anouilh or Sophocles]: Used in my poem to link Colonel Tibbetts of the Enola Gay [The name give to the Boeing B-29 Superfortress bomber, named for Enola Gay Tibbets, the mother of the pilot, Colonel Paul Tibbets, that dropped the H-bomb on Hiroshima] and his refusal to have a marked grave for himself an act that vaguely struck me as a parallel issue of the non-burial of Antigone's brother.

**Aznavour** (Charles) or le grand Charles: Incomparable musician, singer and lyricist who has crystallized for us love and lovers.

**"Believers, Atheists and Moralists"**: This poem tries to encapsulate the pivotal concept that: not believing in absolutes [such as of divinities, of laws etc...] does not equate immorality.

**"Bewitched"**: One of the characters that came to my mind about the mindless and sometimes reckless use of the world of publicity ["Advertising Universe"] especially in the figure of her husband's persona in the series. It is only when you read that the earliest uses and adaptations of this industry were for the selling of the support for World War I, that a chill goes down your spine as to the potential amorality or even immorality of the profession.

**Brel** (Jacques): Belgian born singer who captured life with, at times, heart wrenching lyricism. Such as in "Ne me quitte pas," whose lyrics are the source of several of my poems and in this collection gave me the imagery needed for a poem about the precious—even if mundane—items from the person you love: These items, thus acting the role of Totems.

**Calvados**: An apple eau-de-vie [distillate] which substitutes very well for rum on a Baba.

**Camus** (Albert): I quoted this passage from his play "Caligula" to give a backdrop to this fawn following his mother across a road, while a car could be heard coming around the corner. Camus' figure is also in the background in the "Refusal" of Abraham since the philosopher wrote a powerful pamphlet explaining his stand against capital punishment. In it, Camus wants us to see the legal concept as a physical act: in this case the head falling off the body of a mass killer. He does not want to intellectualize the relationship of this "murder" in front of his eyes with the academic concept that it makes up for a previous one. He relates that his uncle had enthusiastically travelled to witness the guillotining of the murderer of a whole family: only to be sickened by the sight [the immediacy of the blood] of this legally justifiable act.

**Carly Simon**: Composed music for the movie "Heartburn" about the infidelities of a very successful journalist and his wife's descent into loss of innocence and spousal ideals as it is implied in "Between Venus and Mars."

**Columbus and 1492**: The poem superimposes two historic events that show the best and worst of our specie: the irrepressible need to know [going over the unknown ocean] and fear of the Other [the anti-Semitism in Spain and the treatment of the Island Natives of the New World].

**Côte -d'Ivoire**: Calling the street children "Microbes" is a telling sign of the degradation of life in this country. See Africa

**Couscous**: One of the best places to get this North African dish is the Boulevard Saint Michel area where the couple in the poem had decided to meet again.

**Déambulatoires**: Side walkways on each side of seating area of a church. These are usually lined with small altars. See Saint-Germain-des-Prés.

**Delacroix (Eugène)**: Major painter of the Romantic school, with a vast expansive interest in subject matter: From Classical history to contemporary events. His canvases were explosions of energy and colors. "The Death of Sardanapolus" meets all the criteria of his interest and it even allows the painter to show his technical academic training in the details. Thus the presence of this painting on the cover of a poetry book dealing with some of stark realities of the world and the way art selects what it needs out of reality. See Pixels.

**[le] Départ de Saint-Michel**: Bistrot at the corner of the Seine and the Boulevard Saint-Michel. Perfect meeting place in pre-internet and pre-portable phone days because of its easy reference. Sitting in the proper area of the outside sitting, you have "une vue imprenable" [unobstructed view] of Notre Dame de Paris on its island.

**Drieux (Docteur)**: Character from *The Plague* by Albert Camus. In this man, Camus builds the figure of the knowing consciousness of the overwhelming odds against ultimate success; and like Sisyphus, at his task pushing the boulder, he will nevertheless continue to fight against the death of his fellow human beings: in what Camus sees as one of the greatest appeal of men, their solidarity.

**Endeavor**: The first name of Inspector Morse, a fictional character in the eponymous series of detective novels by British author Colin Dexter. See Morse.

**Exarchopoulos (Adèle):** Young French actress who had, in an interview, a disarmingly candid view of her ease with the explicit sexual scenes of "Blue is the Warmest Color," expressing that she wears her nudity like "clothing." She gives us a glance inside the gates of a lost Paradise.

**Existentialism**: Generally, a philosophy that had invaded the universities of Europe and the nights of the coffee houses in Paris. The tenets of this view of life and living, gave a vigorous independent, more self-driven decision-making outlet to a youth ready to move away from the pre-World War II restrictions of morality and religions. [See Absurdism]

**"Force majeure"**: [Poem] How do you train youths, who obey red lights when in their home town, to learn to be willing to kill another human being? See Viet-Nam.

**Fossey (Dian)**: Woman scientist who quietly observed gorillas in their habitat. In this book I compare her ironic relative safety from these enormous beasts toward her presence among them only to be murdered by poachers.

**Frederick Childe Hassam**: American painter influenced by Claude Monet. The poem deals with the American artist feeling conflicted later in his career by the meaning of this Eurocentric and enormous influence on his art. My poem tries to show that it is a question of intrinsic beauty and its transatlantic recognition and successful transplantation and not a weakness on Hassam's part.

**Gauloises**: Powerful French cigarettes.

**Gide (André)**: French writer who had written extensively about his North African travels at a time when the region was a mystery to most of his readers. Thus he had to use the tools of poetic-prose and inventive lyricism to recreate what he saw and felt. The effort made him remark in his travel notes about the frustration of sight. [See "Evolution and Stasis: Representation(s) of the Maghreb in the Works of Loti, Gide, Camus and Le Clezio. Jean-Yves Solinga

**Gitanes**: Powerful French cigarettes.

**Godot**: Character from a play by Beckett. In this absurdist world we wait for the heralded arrival of a person, Godot, who never comes. Beckett, a native English speaker, it is suggested that the Godot character could be God.

**Grasse**:  Magical city, in magical Provence, that produces the magic that is the perfumes from flowers.

**Haussmann (Baron)**: French Politician responsible for the majestic design of the Grandes Avenues of Paris at the cost of whole segments of the poorer neighborhoods destroyed and their population moved to the suburbs. See Robert Moses

**Hell [the Devil, Lucifer, or Evil]**: They play various role in this book: Lucifer for instance because of his previous privileged place in God's eye. On the other hand, Hell and the concept of the symbol of an absolute punishment is also a perfect foil to examine punishment in a godless universe: Such a "A Special Place in Hell."

**Hugo [Victor]**: Used poetry to deal with injustice with a strong sense of republicanism and solidarity.

**Inquisition**: The beginning of the Jewish diaspora from Spain its co-current event: the departure of Columbus to conquer new worlds all happening within months in 1492.

**Félix, Kir**: a priest recognized as the popularizer of a drink made with a  tart white burgundy and currant extracts.

**Lasken, David**: In his book *The Family* he mentions a tragic ironic twist to the well-meaning help by the allied troops opening up the concentration camps. He describes the documented horrors of the early attempts at feeding the newly freed prisoners only to see some of them die from the shock of ingesting such caloric food.

**[Le] Louvre**: A quasi-religious building, where one gets the impression of seeing the tip of the brush touch a canvas for the last time on these iconic masterpieces. "The Death of Sardanapolus" is so large that you feel as though you are walking through the chaos. Not since Georges-Pierre Seurat and La grande Jatte, and primary colors, did one examine art in this manner. The very enormity and the details of Delacrroix's work make one realize before digital photography and pixels etc... . How our sight re-interprets the world. You realize how the mind, by necessity or estheticism, chooses, intermingle or blocks out [pixels out] pieces of the world.
**"Love and Self-Worth"**: I have a vague, unattributed but intriguing note that was to become this poem. It seems words to this effect were found in the cosmetic box of a distinguished woman's personal estate after her death. I added some interpretation for effect but my purpose is hopefully to allow this woman's love to continue living through this poem.

**Lucifer**: I have chosen to use the concept of the most beautiful fallen angel among the several faces of this figure. Evil's attraction for some is what populates literature and makes it fatalistically and joyfully repeatable as a theme.

**(The) Marlboro [or Lucky Strike] man**: Iconic cigarette advertising over Times Square, New York.

**Manet's Olympia**: See Édouard Manet

**Morse (Inspector), The original British ITV series,** [a fictional character in the eponymous series of detective novels by British author Colin Dexter], starts with the older Inspector's introspective and omnipresent love for music, which stands out as a leitmotif in the series. But it is in his younger incarnation, as Endeavor, [Inspector's first name] that the overlap of reality and art is in the forefront and tested. This blending of reality and art is what interested me and inspired the poem in this collection. More specifically, it is when Endeavor has to reconcile the heavenly talent of an opera singer with her involvement in murders: the earthy side of a Muse. See Endeavor

**Moses (Robert):** Visionary New York city politician and designer of major urban changes to the city and beyond. Some doubt remain as to the "extreme curvatures" of the overpasses on the parkways: in particular the ones leading to beaches like Jones Beach. The persisting common rumor or oblique media explanations is that it was to discourage large urban buses easy access to the pristine Long Island sections. See Haussmann.

**Natan (Bernard):** Early cinematographer and also early pornographer. The greater crime and obscenity, as he is concerned and as the poem proposes, is his denunciation as a Jew and eventual death in the concentration camps.
**Notre Dame de Paris:** She [Because since Victor Hugo's novel the building itself is an incarnation] is a "toile de fond" [a backdrop] in many of the passages in this collection. It is a visual and emotional anchor for not only the faithful but, as shown in passages in this book, an artistic and human statement that transcends religion.

**[l'] Olympia:** This masterpiece by Édouard Manet is a statement that a paint brush, a vision and talent can create more reality than the hordes of tourists pushing in front of its museum location. The contrasts between the whiteness of her nudity, the sheets and her glance make me believe that Manet went to his death a contented artist.

**Orange:** In this Provençal City stands a Roman amphitheater and in the afternoon heat, a previous pastis and sitting in its majestic seats, one feels a kinship with what can be good about mankind: Art as an antidote to Time.

**Paris 1960's:** Student strikes, cobblestones, miniscule hotel rooms, youth and Paris. "Between Note Dame de Paris and a Vieux Calvados" and other poems in this collection make reference to the Paris of the 1970, the student rebellions, the appeal of leftist causes [not unlike in the British University system], the deconstruction of everything such as the nouvelle critique—and relearning how to read texts—and yet, as mentioned in the poem the surprising respect of these rebellious—if not revolutionary—students had for Notre de dame de Paris located just down the street, as though it were from another dimension.

**Pascal (Blaise):** In the "Two Infinites" the philosopher speculates on man's relative standing in the Universe and sees him in the middle of the infinitely small (microbes, atoms) and the worlds among the stars.

**Palliative care:** Strange mix, using lyricism in the dying and death of someone in some counterbalancing attempt at finding remnants of human dignity in a deaf universe.

**Pixels**: (pixelated) There is of course the matter of a difference of spelling of the past participle used as an adjective as in this book's title: pixilated, pixelated. But this word and its derivatives have taken a life of its own. The forms of "crazed" or "confused" are not interesting for use in my poems. It is therefore with the advantage (and protection) of poetic license that I approach my use of it. That is, first as a way to choose, emphasize or hide sections of a picture [which the cover of this book does]. Second, the idea of a pixelated reality, or world, made me think of the realities on top of realities depending on how far into an image (or a thought) one goes. In the title-poem for instance, I envision this iconic picture of the Earth from space and the individual pixel within all the pixels, that make up this tiny bluish ball in the blackness of space, that would be the one of a particular loved person back on Earth. In the specific case of "The Death of Sardanapalus," it seems to me as though Delacroix has recreated the effect he wanted with his strategic arrangement of colors to create the impression of blood, And the black parts of the pixelated canvas on the cover of the book give the overall effect picking and choosing pieces of reality.

**Place Clichy**: 1. Active area, not far from Le Moulin Rouge, which is a metaphor in this collection for the earthier, sensual Paris.

**"Place Clichy: A Movable Feast" [The poem]**: 2. The poetic meter in French is determined by the number of syllables per line of poetry. Therefore "Te souviens-tu à Clichy?" has seven syllables: Hence the reference to it as a seven-meter beat [although just a partial phrase]. If an equivalent metered translation were necessary, it would be the coincidentally similar seven syllables in: "Do you remember Clichy?"

**Posséder [to possess]**: The French and English verb are practically synonymous and yet dangerously different depending on the context or application. I use it at times in English in a more emotive way: To make part of yourself. While in the "Love and Self-Worth" [That was originally written in French, it is the elegant term for sexual possession [not as commonly used in English]]. This woman apparently died never having consummated her desires.

**Pervert [Jacques]**: Wrote some of the most romantic song lyrics of the twentieth century in any language. The epigram in "Enfin... c'est triste" are from "Les feuilles mortes" [Automn Leaves] which inspired the poem and should be heard with the Yves Montand's version.

**[la] Princesse de Clèves**: [by Madame de la Fayette] is considered the first novel worthy of the genre in French literature. It describes, basically virtuous persons, where the wife has one errant relationship with an equally principled aristocrat. The story describes and analyzes the dynamics in dealing with the correct course of action, her feelings, her husband's dignity and happiness: An example of the early psychological novel,

**Ralph Nader**: In this book Mr. Nader is used as an icon of what is meant from an unattributed comment: "People vote... people don't vote... people will live... people will die based on it" in reference to the consequences of whom we elect or don't elect in important moments.

**Reprise**: Used sometimes in the suffixes of my titles: It is to refer to a previous same title but different poem. [See Bernard Natan]

**Renoir**: Reaction to the sensual energy still emanating from this painter's canvases in the "half empty Louvre," especially the ones from his last Muse and model.

**Rambo [John]**: Uncharacteristic of my use of this icon of the rewriting of history by the Viet Nam war apologists: It is the touching scene of the Rambo character with the mother of his ex-comrade and the fragility of the black and white photograph between Rambo's fingers that redeems the first movie.

**Resistance**: Glorious and dangerous attempts by the French maquisards in slowing and disrupting the German occupation. The passages in this book make reference to the abject [and uneven] subjugation of the French population to food and the bare necessities for survival: Collaborationists in the next house, legal and illegal food stamps. And amidst the "grisaille" [gray mist] some French women refused to give up their elegance and social dignity, interpreted as a show of passive resistance.

**Rimbaud (Arthur) [1854-1891]**: "Le dormeur du Val," written about the Franco-Prussian war of 1870. Beautiful words to cleanse the wounds and maybe a literary antidote and warning for the stain of the mindless killing of the following wars [WWI and WWII], as reprisals and continuations of this one.

> Le dormeur du val
> C'est un trou de verdure où chante une rivière,
> Accrochant follement aux herbes des haillons
> D'argent ; où le soleil, de la montagne fière,
> Luit : c'est un petit val qui mousse de rayons.
> Un soldat jeune, bouche ouverte, tête nue,
> Et la nuque baignant dans le frais cresson bleu,
> Dort ; il est étendu dans l'herbe, sous la nue,
> Pâle dans son lit vert où la lumière pleut.
>
> Les pieds dans les glaïeuls, il dort. Souriant comme
> Sourirait un enfant malade, il fait un somme :
> Nature, berce-le chaudement : il a froid.
>
> Les parfums ne font pas frissonner sa narine ;
> Il dort dans le soleil, la main sur sa poitrine,
> Tranquille. Il a deux trous rouges au côté droit.
> The Sleeper in the Valley
>
> It is a green hollow where a river sings
> Hanging wildly herbal rags
> Silver, where the sun, proud mountain
> Shines: it is a little valley foam rays.
>
> A young soldier, mouth open, bareheaded,
> And neck bathed in cool blue watercress,
> Sleeps, he is lying in the grass, under the sky,
> Pale in his green bed where the light rains.

Feet in the gladiolas, he sleeps. smiling as
Smile a sick child, he took a nap:
Nature, cradle it warmly: he is cold.

Perfumes are not his nostrils quiver;
He sleeps in the sun, his hand on his chest,
Quiet. It has two red holes in his right side.

**Saint Germain-des-Prés**: Benedictine Abbey in the center of the Quartier Latin. Background setting for many of my poems.

**Sardanapolus [Sardanapale]**: Legendary king of Assyria whose death is depicted in grandiose format by the Romantic painter Eugène Delacroix.

**"Same time next year"**: Popular play and movie about the mores of the 1970's. It is about a couple married to other partners who decide after their first affair to meet in succeeding years. In this book, Paris plays the role of the room of the movie.

**"Semi-virginal"**: In the book this poem analyses how the intensity of loving someone can obliterate the previous history of that person who himself or herself could carry as emotional baggage: No matter the gender combinations of the past indiscretion.

**Simone de Beauvoir**: Partner of Jean-Paul Sartre and author of one of the early seminal texts on the assertion of women *The Second Sex*. See the Stepford Wives.

**"Stepford Wives"**: The women characters of the movie, of the same name, show us a world of the seeming achievement of complete happiness for men. It is a society where the female partners are completely dedicated to their man's enjoyment of life. See Simone de Beauvoir.

**Strategic Air Command [SAC]**: Men of the U.S. Air Force sitting at radar screens during the height of the cold war with the fate of the world in their "divine" hands.

**"The Wire"**: I have forced myself to watch portion of this series to immerse myself from the safety of my living room [hence the TV control in the poem] in the surreal misery and danger of this show, which gave me the feeling of the strangeness in the parallel world of apartheid.

**Tibbets [Paul, Colonel]**: In charge of the bombing of Hiroshima. Although unapologetic about his actions he did refuse to have a marked grave, See Antigone.

**Totems [du désir] [of desire]**: The idea of the powerful personal value of the most innocuous objects in the person we love's personal life. This is pure human poetry since it cannot be [yet] artificially digitized or reproduced by technology: i.e. How would a computer program understand the value of a lock of hair or favorite blanket? See Jacques Brel.

**Viet Nam War**: Recurring presence in my writing. In this book "The Deer Hunter" whose suffix "redux" in the title is to differentiate it from the movie. See "Force Majeure."

# Index

Titles in bold and first lines in italics.

# ABOUT THE AUTHOR

Jean-Yves Solinga

Jean-Yves was born in Algeria, of French parents, moving to Morocco as a babe in his mother's arms when his father was transferred to Salé: practically across from the Kasbah des Udayas of Rabat. Thereafter, he spent an idyllic youth between Morocco and Southern France. Upon settling in America with his family, at the age of 15, he soon began writing poetry as a teenager: being first published in *A Letter Among Friends* along with John Norman of New London, CT. After leaving College, Jean-Yves began a successful career in teaching and lecturing. He holds a doctorate in French on the representation of the Maghrebian [North African] landscape found in the texts by Pierre Loti, André Gide, Albert Camus and Jean-Marie Le Clézio.

Since his retirement he has published several books of poetry: *Clair-Obscur of the Soul* (2008), *Clair-obscur de l'âme* [in French] (2008), *In the Shade of a Flower* (2009), *Landscape of Envies* (2010), *Words Made of Silk* (2011), *Impressions of Reality* (2013). His books offer a singularly unique view of mankind's reflection through the prism of the lyrical language and the quasi impressionist imagery of his poetry. "At times, some passages are examples of the translation of the human condition into pure thought" writes Michael Linnard.

He has been a featured speaker at the Alliance Française of New Haven and Hartford. Presented at the Center of the Teaching of French at Yale University and Southern Connecticut State University on the use of poetry in language studies. Published in "Art et poésie" edited by the renowned French poet Jean-Claude George. He has read at the Poetry Institute of New Haven, Wesleyan University book store, the Cantab Lounge in Cambridge, the Blue Star Café in Providence, the Guilford Green Barn. He has featured at the Bank Square Bookstore and Arts café in Mystic, the Hygienic and the Bean and leaf in New London. He has co-featured at the Mystic Art Gallery, and at the Harriet Beecher Stowe Center on the theme of social justice in poetry. Jean-Yves has had poems published in the *Lay Bare the Canvas: New England Poets on Art* by the Free Poet Collective Ekpharsis Project at the New Britain museum, and the annual *Little Red Tree Anthology*. His poetry has been nominated three times for a Pushcart Award.

Jean-Yves Solinga is a poet of immense ability and range whose poetry is truly remarkable. It contains many breathtakingly beautiful and sophisticated poems that reach out to the very limits of the human condition where true art exists. Many facets of his work find inspiration and perspective in his cultural duality. This gives his poems an historical and critical breath. In *Artist in a Pixelated World*, Jean-Yves examines the space that positions the artist in the privileged overlap between reality and art in their various forms.

Photograph taken by: Michael Linnard

www.ingramcontent.com/pod-product-compliance
Lightning Source LLC
Chambersburg PA
CBHW080531090426
42733CB00015B/2549

* 9 7 8 1 9 3 5 6 5 6 3 1 9 *